Saga of the Samurai: Book 4

# SHINGEN IN COMMAND:

## THE KAI TAKEDA 4 (1549-1558)

Terje Solum . Anders K. Rue

**Brookhurst** Press

First Edition

Printed by Impact Printing, Chino Hills, CA
Translated By Ian Harkness
Edited By Dan Weber
Maps By Jan B. Loa
Designed By Creative Pull, Anaheim, CA

Brookhurst Press
12188 Brookhurst St.
Garden Grove, CA 92840

Phone (714) 636-3580
Fax (714) 636-9150

E-mail: info@sagaofthesamurai.com

Web Site: www.sagaofthesamurai.com

(Title Page)
**Photo TAK 4-1**

Takeda Shingen in camp, preparing to march to war. (Shingen-kô festival in Kôfu).

## DEDICATION

To my long time friend, Trond Sagafos

## ACKNOWLEDGEMENTS

I am extremely grateful to the book's illustrator, Anders K. Rue, for his excellent drawings, and Jan B. Loa who drew the maps. I also wish to express my thanks to Henry Tremblay and his staff at Brookhurst Hobbies for all their assistance. A special thanks goes to the manager of the arts and science department of the *Uma no hakubutsukan* (The Horse Museum) in Yokohama, Murai Fumihiko, for his valuable information. This museum is well worth a visit; it is a must if you want to learn more about horses and horsemanship during the Japanese Middle Ages. I would like to offer the same thank you to the Kaida village in Kiso, Nagano prefecture, for their beautiful Kiso horses – this place is also a must for the true student of the samurai.

## NOTES ON THE TEXT AND PHOTOGRAPHS

The Japanese names in this book are written surname first, in accordance with tradition. Unless stated otherwise, the dates are in keeping with the old Japanese calendar. Japanese vowels will sometimes be distinguished with a diacritical mark, '^.' This indicates that the vowel is twice as long. This is to differentiate between certain family names, such as Môri and Mori, and to facilitate pronunciation. Where source material indicates different names for the same individual or location the name occurring most commonly will appear in the text followed by any other names in parenthesis. In addition, to avoid confusion, the terms "family" and "clan" are used interchangeably throughout the book.

All photographs in the text were taken on location in Japan by the author.

**Terje Solum** has for more than a decade studied the history of Japan, specializing in the *Sengoku Jidai* period. In addition to having studied the Japanese language at an institute near Nagoya, he has traveled all over Japan in search of information related to the samurai. The *Saga of the Samurai* series is his first major book project.

**Anders K. Rue** is a commercial artist living and working in Norway. Working within a wide range of styles, for the last 5 years he has concentrated on drawings recreating historical events. His best known art is found in the the book *The Kings of Norway* and a newly published version of *Snorre*, the epic saga of the Vikings.

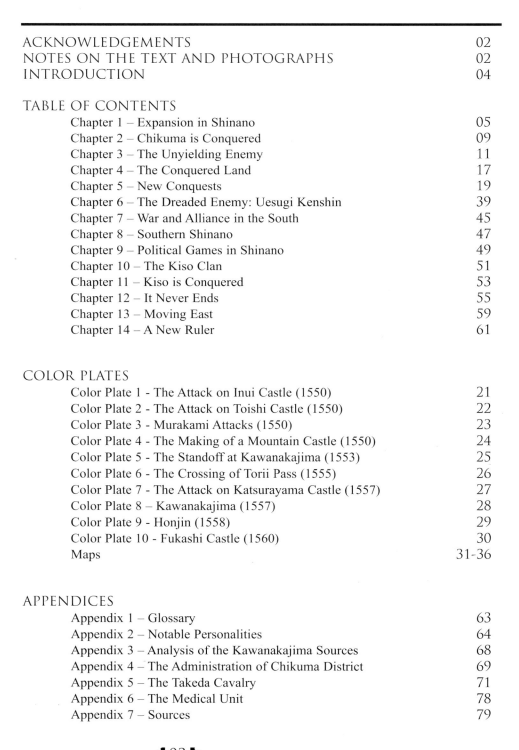

# INTRODUCTION

**B**ook four in the *Saga of the Samurai* series is a continuation of the story of Takeda Shingen and his life and accomplishments between 1549 and 1558. Of the numerous military campaigns and battles waged by Shingen during this period, perhaps the best known are the conflicts with Uesugi Kenshin from Kasugayama Castle in Echigo, a lord who slowly but surely became involved in a long struggle against the Takeda.

The conflict with Uesugi led to a war that lasted for more ten years, from 1553 to 1564. During this period, the armies of Shingen and Kenshin clashed several times on a wide plain known as Kawanakajima, in the northern part of Shinano. We will study accounts of the battles and military campaigns at Kawanakajima in this book. We will also introduce the reader to the *onsen* (hot springs) regions of Kai, which were used not only for the rehabilitation of injured soldiers, but also for recreational purposes. There will also be a discussion of the administration of the Chikuma (Tsukama) district in Shinano, as well as a closer look at the cavalry of the Takeda clan, especially their horses.

## SUMMARY

**I**n the three previous *Saga of the Samurai* books, we became acquainted with the first generations of the Takeda clan and the region that they governed, the Kai province. Around 500 years of family history has been covered, including the two most prominent leaders of the early 16th century: Takeda Nobutora in book two, and Takeda Shingen in book three. These books have given us insight into the workings of a samurai clan during the Sengoku period. However, we are far from finished with Takeda Shingen. Book three ended with Shingen's campaign of 1548, where he suffered his first defeat at Uedahara, but from which he managed to recover. This fourth book continues the story of Shingen's life and exploits as well as the history of the Takeda Clan of Kai, taking up the thread again in late 1548.

# Chapter 1 – Expansion in Shinano

## NEW TREASURES

In all probability Shingen's numerous military excursions had consumed considerable resources, and financial necessity led to the introduction of new taxes in 1549. The first was levied in May, and was aimed at the upper castes of the samurai. The tax was called the *utokusen* (also *utokuyaku* or *tokuyakusen*), which might be translated as "surtax." Under certain circumstances, Shingen could demand extra taxes from the upper-class samurai, namely those with the titles of Sagami *no Kami*, Dewa *no Kami* and Ise *no Kami*. How the upper classes reacted to the new tax is unknown, but it is reasonable to assume that those affected were less than enthusiastic over the increased taxation.

In November of the same year, Shingen held negotiations with Oyamada Nobuari, a Takeda general who ruled more or less independently over a large section of the Tsuru district in Kai known as the Gunnai region. The result of the meeting was a tax known as *karyôsen*, which might be translated as a "correctional fine" and was a duty paid when the law was broken. It is unknown how serious an offense needed to be for a *karyôsen* to be levied. The size of the fine and who was responsible for levying it is also uncertain. Perhaps it was the *gundai* or *jitô* (officials) who were responsible, or the amount might have been determined by Shingen. The new tax applied to farmers and priests within Gunnai, the region administrated by the Oyamada family. The fines probably applied to all the Takeda territories. Not surprisingly, the population was not pleased with the new tax.

## 1549 – REBELLION IN SAKU

1548 had ended. It had been an eventful year for Shingen. He had experienced his first defeat in battle, but returned stronger than before. The Takeda clan now dominated Suwa, Saku, and the northern part of the Ina district. North of these districts, however, powerful families awaited Shingen and his army. During 1548, Shingen was made painfully aware of his strong opposition in the north. His opposition, Murakami and Ogasawara, soon realized they could not oppose Takeda alone. They therefore allied themselves with other families in Shinano, which was one of the primary causes of Shingen's defeat at Uedahara. As soon as the districts in Shinano were under Takeda's control, it became necessary to place competent commanders in all forts of strategic significance. The conquered lands were given as rewards to his soldiers, and the areas were gradually incorporated into Takeda Shingen's expanding empire. Clans that swore allegiance to Shingen were expected to send hostages to Tsutsujigasaki as insurance for their continued loyalty. Those who had chosen to resist to the end were annihilated. It was primarily their lands that were dealt out to vassals, both new recruits and veterans.

As spring approached, new military operations were planned. The spring offensive of 1549 took place in the western part of the Chikuma district of Shinano. Kiso-guchi and the Torii Pass were the gateway to the Kiso Valley. The area held by the Kiso clan was a strategically significant junction. In order to reach Fukushima Castle, it was necessary to take and hold the famous Nakasendô road. The Nakasendô road led to several provinces in the west and had been of great strategic importance to Shingen for some time. Unfortunately for Shignen, the rulers of the area were the Kiso clan, who could trace their roots back to the renowned samurai, Minamoto Yoshiie (1039-1106). They were a proud and noble clan who lived in the mountains of the Chikuma district. Shingen knew it would not be an easy task to conquer the Kiso lands.

Of the first of Takeda's invasions into Kiso, the historical source *Kôyô gunkan* has the following to say: "in the middle of April 1549, the Takeda army invaded the territories of Kiso, and the districts of Hirazawa and Narai were burned. The army went through Torii Pass and approached Yabuhara (Sawahara), where a battle was fought with no clear victor." Since the result of the battle was uncertain, Takeda pulled his army back to Suwa. Another reference reporting on the events in Narai and Hirasawa indicated that Takeda came into conflict with the Narai and Niekawa clans who resided there, but little information is available on the outcome of these battles.

Fukuyo Castle in the Ina district experienced a renaissance. A *kuwaire* (or ground-breaking) ceremony (also referred to as a *kuwadate*) was held within the ruins of the castle on July 15, 1549 signifying the castle's reconstruction had officially begun. Fukuyo, which subsequently seems to have been referred to as Minowa, was to become an important base in the Ina district

**Photo TAK 4-3**

Fukuyo Castle's renaissance came under the Takeda, and served from from that point on as a base castle in Kami Ina. Looking over to the northern compound from the first *honmaru*.

for Takeda. It also served as a headquarters for military forays into the whole of Shinano, both to the south and to the north. The fortress was rather large and divided into two sections – the "northern fortress," and the "southern fortress." From north to south, the entire stronghold measured around 450 meters. The southern fortress covered an area about 200 meters long, and about 350 meters wide. The northern fortress stretched about 250 meters in length, and

**Photo TAK 4-4**

Standing on the second *honmaru* of Fukuyo Castle, looking up towards the first *honmaru* (main compound), Ina district.

**Photo TAK 4-5**

Standing on the valley floor in Ina, looking up towards the ridge that comprises the Fukuyo Castle. In the background we can see parts of the Akaishi Mountains. Ina district, Nagano prefecture.

about 100 meters in width. Natural river dikes surrounded the fortress, and several moats had been excavated, making the fortress a formidable obstacle. It was extremely difficult to assault, a fact the Takeda army had already discovered. In combination with Ryûgasaki and Takatô, it formed an important barrier between Ina and Suwa. Shingen had ensured his conquered territories were well protected by the crossroads these fortresses created.

Murakami Yoshikiyo had been victorious at Uedahara in 1548, subsequently attacking and conquering several of the Takeda clan's castles in the Saku district. Only a few months later, these fortresses were again under the control of the Takeda. Murakami, however, was not yet out of the running. In the fall of 1549, he decided once again to challenge Takeda's bases in Saku. Several clans returned to the fray, and news of their opposition reached Shingen. Shingen was residing at Takashima Castle (this Takashima Castle is not the same as the one located in Suwa today) in Suwa when the news of problems arrived. He ordered full mobilization, and on August 23 set off for Saku. On August 26, his army arrived at Sakuraiyama Castle, which remained under his control. On August 28, the Takeda army pillaged and burned the area around Oidachi before continuing on their journey. On September 1, they made camp at Sagibayashi. Three days later, the Takeda army attacked Hirahara Castle (also known as Urigoya Castle) in Komoro, burning it to the ground. On September 21, the Takeda army returned to Tsutsujigasaki. Little is known of the campaign of 1549 in Saku. It is said that the Mochizuki, Tomono, Ashida, and Yoda clans, who initially supported Murakami, eventually concluded that the war was lost, and further resistance would lead to their collective ruin. They surrendered, swearing their support of the Takeda clan. This battle permanently eliminated Murakami's influence in the Saku district.

**Illustration 4-1.**

A *teppô ashigaru* taking aim and ready to fire. During the 1550s the Japanese *teppô* gradually increased in popularity and every lord wanted this new weapon. This *ashigaru* wears a simple *okegawa nimai-dô* (*nimai* = two section/plates) with a metal *jingasa* on his head. *Teppô* manufacturing styles varied during the later half of the Sengoku Jidai and most were named after the town in which they were produced.

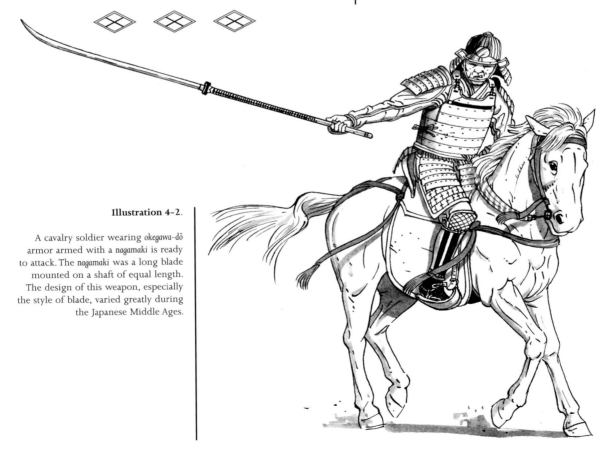

**Illustration 4-2.**

A cavalry soldier wearing *okegawa-dô* armor armed with a *nagamaki* is ready to attack. The *nagamaki* was a long blade mounted on a shaft of equal length. The design of this weapon, especially the style of blade, varied greatly during the Japanese Middle Ages.

# Chapter 2 – Chikuma is Conquered

## SHINGEN CHALLENGES OGASAWARA

Shingen had established a base at Murai Castle about 8 kilometers south of Hayashi Castle in the Chikuma district, intending to use it as his headquarters in the coming campaign. Work on the castle was begun on October 4, 1548, quickly preparing it for use. The castle was located in an area Shingen captured from Ogasawara Nagatoki during the battle at Shiojiri. With the successful outcome of this battle, Shingen gained control over territories on both sides of the pass. Once these areas were conquered, giving him control of the southern part of the Chikuma district, Shingen continued to push northward towards Hayashi Castle. He devoted most of 1549 to reinforcing the defenses of previously conquered areas, the main exception being his battles in Saku against the Murakami clan and their allies. Shingen, however, was intent on new campaigns in Shinano. As 1550 advanced, his general staff continued to lay plans.

At the end of June 1550, the order to mobilize was given. On July 3, Shingen set out from Tsutsujigasaki, reaching Murai Castle in Chikuma on July 10. The entire army was consolidated, and a war council was held. Early in the evening of July 15 (or July 13, according to another source), Takeda's troops carried out a surprise attack on Inukai, one of Hayashi Castle's auxiliary forts, which lay about 1.5 kilometers northwest of Fukashi Castle. So swift was the attack that the defenders were unable to organize their defenses in time. By eight o'clock that evening the fort had fallen. The traditional cry of victory was heard ringing out from the fort's parade grounds. According to sources, 10,000 men took part. Most of the army returned to Murai shortly afterwards.

The soldiers defending the auxiliary forts Fukashi, Okada, Kirihara and Yamabe seem to have completely lost their will to fight, fleeing in total disarray upon hearing the Takeda army was on the march. The commander at Shimadachi fort, Shimadachi Ukon, and the commander at Asama fort, Akazawa Saemon, surrendered without resistance. Ogasawara Nagatoki fled shortly afterwards to Hirase Castle, a little north of Hayashi. Still fearing Takeda pursuit, he immediately set out again for the Hanishina district, where Murakami Yoshikiyo resided, and where he hoped he would be safe. The benefits of capturing the tiny fort at Inukai on the evening of July 15 were far greater than Shingen could have hoped for. Almost the entire Chikuma district fell under the rule of the Takeda clan, virtually without resistance, and Shingen dispatched troops to secure the abandoned forts in the area. Only the region on the other side of the Torii Pass remained under the dominion of the local lord of the Kiso clan. Consequently, many clans were enlisted into Shingen's army. They were organized into *kuni-shû* (country units), but their true loyalties were probably somewhat divided. Therefore, all newly allied clans were required to send hostages to ensure their cooperation. If a clan chose to revolt, the prisoners, who were almost always members of the family, were killed. The methods were often brutal: they could be hanged, boiled alive, decapitated, or crucified. The latter became extremely popular after Christianity was introduced by missionaries in the late 1540s.

While Hayashi Castle was being destroyed, Shingen ordered that Fukashi Castle should be restored and strengthened. The *Kuwadate* ceremony was held on July 19 on the parade grounds. According to the source *Kôyô gunkan*, the reconstruction began on July 23, under the direction of Yamamoto Kansuke. Fukashi was to serve as the main headquarters for the continuing campaigns further north in Shinano.

In April of 1550, Shingen's general, Komai Kôhakusai, is said to have contacted the Nishina clan of the Azumi district, who were under the leadership of Nishina Dôgai Moriyasu, convincing them to change sides and join Takeda. At the time, the Azumi district was still under the theoretical control of the Ogasawara clan. Despite this, fear of Shingen seems to have spread, causing many of the smaller clans to surrender without resistance. Many families defected to Takeda, including the Akazawa, Banzai, Mimura, Nishimaki, Shimadachi, and Yamabe clans, as well as some former *hatamoto* families of the Ogasawara clan; the latter included such groups as the Inukai, Hirase, Kariya, and Omi clans. It should be pointed out that the affiliations between the families of the Chikuma and Azumi districts and the Takeda clan were rather loose. Opposition from one or two families might rapidly spread to involve the entire central region of Shinano.

Shingen was aware of this problem, and knew that both a solid defense and good leadership would be required to govern the region. Shingen therefore assigned Baba Nobuharu, a very loyal and competent general, to govern Fukashi on both the military and administrative levels. It appears that the region around Matsumoto, including Fukashi, became a part of Shingen's *kurairi-chi*, namely a region under Shingen's direct control. Because of its location, Fukashi became an administrative center as well as a storage and production area. For the Takeda clan, Fukashi became one of their most important fortresses in central Shinano, helping to establish the clan in the province. It would

henceforth be very difficult indeed for the remaining clans in Shinano to stop this *tsunami* from the south. Perhaps Murakami might have been able to slow down Takeda, but his clan could not manage it without allies - a fact Murakami Yoshikiyo was well aware of.

**Illustration 4-4**.

A samurai on horseback wearing *okegawa-dô* armor armed with a *naginata*. Favored by warrior monks and women, the *naginata* had a longer shaft and a more curved blade than the *nagamaki*. This warrior carries a *tachi* sword in his sash – cutting edge down.

# Chapter 3 - The Unyielding Enemy

## THE ATTACK ON TOISHI CASTLE, 1550

Not long after the majority of Chikuma was occupied, Shingen started to lay plans for an attack against Murakami in the Hanishina district, northeast of Chikuma. Shingen was aware of Murakami's influence in Shinano, presumably thinking that if he could crush Murakami most of his opposition in Shinano would surrender with little resistance. In July, he held discussions with his general, Sanada Yukitaka; Shingen had promised land in Saku to Sanada if he managed to capture Toishi Castle in the Chiisagata district.

An auxiliary fort of Katsurao Castle about eight kilometers to the southeast, Toishi guarded a strategically important area. Because of this, no further progress could be made in the direction of Katsurao before Toishi was taken. Shingen's promise provided Yukitaka with ample motivation, and he departed eagerly on August 5, 1550, along with a vanguard force led by Nagasaka Torafusa. Murakami, however, did not intend to give up without a fight. Toishi was packed with soldiers, and he commanded these troops personally as the Takeda army approached. Murakami was well-prepared, for while Shingen had been occupied with the battles in Chikuma he had made preparations to defend his territory against invasion. He had anticipated that once Shingen had crushed the resistance in Chikuma he would resume his efforts to expand northward.

**Photo TAK 4-6**

The entrance to the path leading up to Toishi Castle can be seen on the right just past the sign. Toishi is located on the mountaintop to the right.

**Photo TAK 4-7**

The path leading up to the main castle. Toishi Castle was known for its steep sides, and after walking up there, without enemies firing down at me, I can truly say that Toishi must have been a formidable fortress.

**Photo TAK 4-8**

Toishi Castle seen from the honmaru of Sanada Castle. Further in the background you can see parts of Ueda city.

**Photo TAK 4-9 (above) & TAK 4-10 (above right)**

This is Toishi Castle's *honmaru*. During the Takeda invasions, the castle functioned as a support castle for the Murakami clan. Trickery used by the Takeda general, Sanada Yukitaka, in 1551 captured the castle.

**Photo TAK 4-11**

Toishi Castle's mountain as seen from the village below.

Murakami was, to some extent, frightened of Shingen's army. He knew he stood no chance of standing alone against the mighty Takeda clan. He therefore engaged the majority of the remaining independent families in Shinano as allies. One of these feudal overlords was the brave, but at that time defeated lord, Ogasawara Nagatoki. Ogasawara had escaped to Katsurao Castle after the defeat in Chikuma, and now stood alongside Yoshikiyo within Toishi's walls. In addition to Ogasawara members of the Inoue, Takanashi, Kiyono (one source calls this Seino), and Terao clans stood ready against the Takeda. Altogether, Murakami had 5,000 soldiers at his disposal.

However, before Shingen's main forces arrived at Toishi they attacked several minor fortresses. One of these was Wada, where it was mentioned that on August 10, extra *ashigaru* troops (infantry) were sent in against the castle. The defenders of Wada fortress soon lost their nerve and fled. On August 19, Shingen and his army of around 8,000 men (another source says 10,000) were on their way over

Daimon Pass, making camp at Nagakubo. The Takeda army progressed slowly but surely towards Toishi. On the 22nd of August, Shingen sent Imai Tôzaemon (or Shinzaemon) and Yasuda Shikibushôyû ahead of the main force to the area around Toishi not only to study the terrain and enemy defenses, but also to prepare for his arrival. The following day, Ôi Nobutsune, Hara Toratane, and Yokota Takatoshi (or Takamatsu) were also sent to scout the area. At 8 o'clock on the morning of August 27, the Takeda army set out from Nagakubo Castle, swinging southwards towards Unnokuchi. The army camped by Mukonohara. As Shingen looked north, the Chikuma River lay before him. Further north still, beyond the river, lay Toishi Castle. On August 28 the Takeda finally arrived in the neighborhood of the castle itself.

Shingen's main camp was established in a place called Yaburi, an area below Toishi, while the soldiers surrounded the *yamashiro* (mountain castle). At noon the following day, Shingen traveled to the front, to view Toishi Castle personally. A brief exchange between divisions of archers took place, but no direct attack was launched on the castle itself. The main attack did not begin until six in the evening of September 9. In order to reach the base of Toishi, the troops had to pass through a narrow valley, where the Takeda vanguard came under heavy enemy fire. Groups of archers and spear-throwing soldiers made progress difficult for Shingen's men. It made a very poor start for Shingen's campaign against Murakami, taking his soldiers longer than planned to gain control over the area around the base of the castle.

Violent battles around Toishi continued for days as the enemy's defenses were constantly put under pressure. Reportedly, *teppô* (matchlock) were used by the Takeda army during the attack on Toishi. It was claimed that the *teppô* division was led by Oyamada Dewa *no Kami* Nobuari. If *teppô* were actually employed during the attack on Toishi, they were probably not Japanese firearms, but weapons imported from China. While the Chinese had used some type of firearms of various quality long before the Japanese produced their own, the quality was rather poor.

It soon became clear that the Takeda army had to find weaknesses in the castle's defense if the campaign was to be successful. Each attack ended with heavy losses followed by a retreat. When the attackers attempted to scale the steep sides of the mountain castle they were constantly bombarded with large stones and showers of arrows. A decisive Takeda victory appeared beyond reach. The castle defenses were not the only obstacle they faced; the cold September wind and nightly frost made life even more difficult for the Takeda soldiers.

Shingen initially hoped Toishi's defenses would collapse quickly so he could continue his campaign. His primary goal was to attack Yoshikiyo's castle, Katsurao, but he knew Toishi was strategically important and needed to be taken before he could proceed. As the attack bogged down, the possibility of a quick victory began to appear more and more remote. Shingen assumed that Yoshikiyo was leading the defense from the walls of Toishi as the battle wore on. However, he was greatly mistaken, because Murakami Yoshikiyo had left Toishi (although the precise point of his departure is uncertain). It is possible he had left shortly before Takeda surrounded the castle. Yoshikiyo had not left out of fear, but to mobilize a rescue force to challenge Takeda, create chaos in the enemy ranks, and break the siege.

But Yoshikiyo was not the only one who was scheming. In the hope of weakening the coalition army, Shingen had ordered Sanada Yukitaka to recruit some of the local lords from the other side. He had some limited success with his mission because the Kiyono clan (from the Hanishina district) turned up in the Takeda camp at four in the afternoon of September 1, and the Suda clan (from the Takai district) appeared on the 19th of September. Shingen also received some less pleasant news. On September 23, he learned from Kiyono that Takanashi Masayori, who had (up until that point) supported the Takeda clan, had switched sides and joined the alliance with Murakami. Both clans had joined forces and were now attacking Terao Castle. Since the commander of Terao supported Takeda, Shingen decided to dispatch Sanada Yukitaka with troops to come to his assistance. Yukitaka managed to create confusion in the ranks of the attackers, forcing them to retreat. Yukitaka returned to the main camp at Toishi on the evening of September 29.

During Yukitaka's absence Shingen had continued the siege. Little progress was being made, so on September 30 a war-council was held in Shingen's *honjin* (headquarters). Shingen and his generals discussed the latest developments, finally reaching the conclusion that their goals were unachievable at that time. If they remained much longer, they risked attack by any number of enemy troops. Victory had eluded Shingen for now, and early in the morning of October 1, the army began its march back to Suwa. The retreat was not missed by Murakami, who wanted the last word in this battle. In the evening, Takeda's *shingari-tai* (rear guard) was attacked by Murakami's forces. The rear guard force of the Takeda army met with the Murakami forces, but after a short fight managed to fend them off. Shingen's main forces camped at Mochizuki, where they were harassed by torrential rain throughout the night. The following day, October 2, the army passed through Daimon Pass and entered Suwa. At six in the evening, they established camp at Yugawa. Shingen entered Uehara Castle the following day. On October 6, he set out for Tsutsujigasaki.

## ADDITIONAL INFORMATION ON THE BATTLE AT TOISHI

One source claims that Murakami Yoshikiyo was able to gather around 4,000 cavalry troops to break the siege on Toishi Castle. According to the source, Murakami led them to the rear of Shingen's main encampment and attacked the enemy camp on the morning of September 23. At the same time, Murakami's troops attacked Shingen's *honjin* at Toishi, forcing him into a desperate fight on two fronts. However, details of this report do not agree with the details in other reports of the battle at Toishi. It is therefore not clear what actually took place at the foot of the castle. It is mentioned that Yoshikiyo left Toishi Castle to assemble an army to attack the enemy camp. The figure of 4,000 cavalry appears to be a rather high estimate of the number of troops who participated in the attack.

**Illustration 4-5.**

A samurai armed with two swords prepares himself for the oncoming enemy. To be able to fight well with a weapon in each hand was a strong point over any enemy. Both samurai wear tachi swords, *haidate* (thigh-guards), and *okegawa-dō* armor.

## REFLECTIONS AND NEW PLANS

Shingen's campaign against Toishi had become an expensive affair, especially considering the main goals were eventually abandoned. Altogether, around 1,000 soldiers were said to have been killed, among them two of Oyamada Nobuyoshi's captains: Ozawa Shikibu and Watanabe Izumo *no Kami*. Worst of all for Shingen was the loss of a loyal general of many years, General Yokota Takatoshi. Takatoshi - who had fought bravely to the end - was killed on the evening of October 1, serving in the rearguard which came under attack (another source says he was killed around September 23). Shingen had suffered his second defeat, yet again at the hands of Murakami Yoshikiyo. What was he to do?

Although it was only a minor setback for Shingen, the consequences of the defeat could be serious. He could only hope that his enemies would not exploit the situation. Shingen chose to bide his time, but his archenemy soon turned up again. Yoshikiyo intended to wring every drop from his advantage. On October 9, his army attacked the Iwamurada (Iwamurata) estate in Saku, burning it to the ground.

Ogasawara Nagatoki, who had participated in the defense of Toishi, had also witnessed Shingen's defeat. Not surprisingly, he too wanted to exploit the victory. By October 21, he had mustered an army near Himuro in the Azumi district southwest of Toishi. Together with Murakami, he intended to retake Fukashi, which lay about five kilometers from his current position. The army attacked and overran the fortresses of Shimadachi and Hirase, and was making preparations to continue on to Fukashi when they heard on October 23 the Takeda army was on its way. Shingen was not about to stand idly by and watch his enemies regain the territories he

had conquered, instead sending Obu Toramasa and others to challenge his enemies. Murakami, who was also on the warpath, heard of the movements of the Takeda army, and broke off his campaign, retiring to Katsurao. Ogasawara now stood in a most unenviable position - alone against Takeda. With his men fleeing into the mountains Nagatoki finally retreated to Nakatô Castle. Satisfied with the news of his enemies' actions, Shingen recalled his troops.

Murakami's actions in October were a setback, but he did not remain quiet for long. On November 8, his army captured Komoro Castle, south of Toishi. On November 13, Yoshikiyo's troops attacked the forts of Nozawa and Sakuraiyama in the Saku district, and set them on fire. Many villages in the area suffered similar fates. The Terao family, which had defected to the Takeda camp, now felt Murakami's wrath. Women and children of the Terao clan were massacred. Shingen replied by moving to his border fortress against Saku in Shinano, Wakamiko Castle in Kai. After this he sent his general, Komai Masatake, against Unnokuchi in Saku, but no confrontation with Murakami's troops followed. Perhaps Murakami's army retired after its pillaging. On November 19, Shingen returned home to Tsutsujigasaki.

## SANADA YUKITAKA CAPTURES TOISHI

Shingen chose to stay in Kai for the winter. The defeat at Toishi had to be digested, and other activities were now given priority. On December 7 of the same year a feast was held at the manor in Kôfu. A *genpuku* ceremony was held for Shingen's first-born son, Yoshinobu. In February 1551, Shingen visited the Asama temple in Kai and presented them with a letter in which it was written they were to receive land as a token of gratitude for his success in Shinano, and to guarantee the gods would ensure his future fortune in war. To visit temples that had close ties before and after a campaign was a normal practice for Shingen.

In May 1551 Shingen again busied himself with plans aimed at vanquishing the Murakami clan. The promise of land made to Sanada Yukitaka for his allegiance in the campaign against Murakami in the autumn of 1550 had whetted Yukitaka's appetite for action. The promise involved considerable tracts of land within the Suwa and Chiisagata districts, worth roughly 1,000 *kanmon*. Shingen's first attempt at capturing Toishi had ended in a fiasco, so he now gave Yukitaka a free hand in attempting to capture the castle. A task Yukitaka took seriously.

The first thing Yukitaka did was to attempt to split the coalition Murakami Yoshikiyo had made. One of Yohsikiyo's most powerful allies was Takanashi Masayori. The Takanashi family

was one of the few powerful families left in Shinano, so breaking the alliance would be a great tactical success for Yukitaka. He contacted Masayori, and managed to convince him to change sides. Once the Takanashi leader had allied himself with the Takeda, Yukitaka could move on to the next stage of his plans.

Instead of attempting to attack and storm an almost impregnable fortress like Shingen had done Yukitaka's strategy was more devious. The promise of gold or land could always lure men to betray their masters. Yukitaka managed to make contact with soldiers inside the castle walls and using that promise he convinced many of them to change sides. Once this was achieved the rest was easy. The betrayers opened the castle gates and Yukitaka's troops stormed in and captured the castle.

One important reason for Yukitaka's victory at Toishi was the fact that in all probability Murakami Yoshikiyo had grown arrogant and complacent after his victory against Shingen the year before. There were no longer as many soldiers stationed at Toishi, so when Yukitaka turned up with his army the defenders found themselves hopelessly outnumbered. Combine this with the bribed traitors inside the garrison's ranks and Toishi Castle's time as an auxiliary fort in defense of Katsurao was finally over.

But where was Murakami Yoshikiyo? It is noted in one source (belonging to the Ogasawara family) that when Shingen invaded Shinano in March 1551, Yoshikiyo fled north toward the Kawanakajima Plain. But when Toishi fell on May 26, Yoshikiyo is said to have been staying at Katsurao. Yoshikiyo had kept calm during the siege, no doubt thinking Sanada's forces did not pose any immediate and serious threat to the castle. It is possible Yoshikiyo thought that Sanada's force would not be able to capture Toishi without a long siege. This would seem a logical conclusion considering Shingen's powerful army had not been successful the year before. He therefore gave the order to mobilize to assist Toishi only if necessary, believing the castle's forces could defend themselves until reinforcements arrived.

Just as Yukitaka had been successful in getting families in the area to change sides, so too was Yamamoto Kansuke out on a similar mission. Large sums of money had been given to families in the area around Toishi, and within a brief period of time the front was pushed further north, nearer to Katsurao. Bit by bit Murakami Yoshikiyo found himself more and more isolated, but this wily general was not without initiative, and sought alliances further to the north. The most important of these was with the lord of Kasugayama Castle in Echigo, Nagao Kagetora, better known as Uesugi Kenshin.

**Illustration 4-6.**

Two *ashigaru* carry their lord in a *kago* (palanquin). When not on horseback, or due to illness, the lord was carried in a *kago*. Several styles of *kago* were in use during the Japanese Middle Ages.

**Illustration 4-7.**

Women, typically a wife or concubine, were usually carried in a *kago* between castles and mansions. They usually traveled in a closed *kago* like the one illustrated when on a journey across the countryside. Obviously, *kago* bearers needed to be quite strong.

# Chapter 4 - The Conquered Land

## SHINANO

**Illustration 4-8.**

A samurai with a *no-tachi* (extra long) sword. Too long to carry on the left side, this sword was usually worn on the back. In addition to his *no-tachi*, this warrior also carries a *tachi*, and a *wakizashi* or a *tantô* (dagger) – he is ready for battle. He wears a suit of *okegawa nimai-dô* armor.

Shinano province was roughly three times larger than Kai. Present-day Shinano is called Nagano prefecture and encompasses an area of 13,584 square kilometers; Yamanashi prefecture (Kai province) is in comparison only 4,464 square kilometers in area. As far as the size of the respective populations is concerned figures from 1835 list Shinano having a population of 808,073, while Kai province had 318,474 inhabitants. If we consider rice, the most important production unit for food, measured in *koku* (where one *koku* represented the annual consumption of rice per person, roughly 180 liters); then in 1835 Shinano had an annual production of 767,788 *koku, while* Kai produced only 312,159 *koku*. In addition to a large land area, which provided the basis for substantial rice production, Shinano province was also rich with mineral resources.

Shinano's large land area, food production, population, and ample mineral resources provided an alluring target to its voracious and powerful Kai neighbor. Shingen seems to have made the right choice in attacking to the north, since the Imagawa family had in the previous decade tightened its grip on the Suruga and Tôtômi provinces in the south. Uesugi lay to the east and even Hôjô had become powerful. To the west, behind the southern alps, lay the Ina district, part of Shinano province. To strike out toward these areas in Ina, Shingen had to first conquer the Suwa district, which also lay in Shinano. This he managed to do, over time conquering more and more of the province.

Much of the explanation for Shingen's success lay in the fact that there was no lord in Shinano province powerful enough to unify the province under one banner. Instead only a handful of medium-sized clans governed more or less independently within Shinano. Lacking strong alliances, these clans were very vulnerable. This scenario provided Shingen with great opportunity as long as he played his cards right; and that is exactly what he managed to do – although there were some minor setbacks along the way. After ten years of campaigning in Shinano, the Takeda clan had managed to take almost five of Shinano's ten districts. However, because Murakami Yoshikiyo had not been defeated nor his Katsurao Castle captured, Shingen was by no means finished with his campaigns in the north. Murakami still remained a threat in Shinano, and as has been mentioned before, Shingen had previously suffered defeat at the hands of this lord on two separate occasions. This fact was undoubtedly painful to Shingen, and we may surmise that he felt a strong desire to be rid of Murakami once and for all. Shingen was very pleased with Sanada Yukitaka's capture of Toishi Castle, which restored some of Shingen's lost honor. But there were still large areas of Shinano still not under the dominion of the Takeda clan. It would not be long before the Takeda army marched north again.

**Illustration 4-9.**

Two ashigaru with *take-gusoku* (bamboo armor) defend a samurai who is fending off enemies with his bow. Both *ashigaru* wear armor produced in the thousands during the 16th century. Typically, its owner – usually a farmer – most likely produced the bamboo armor himself. The samurai with the bow wears and old style Ô-*yoroi* armor.

**Illustration 4-10.**

A samurai armed with a *tanjû* (short gun). It was not until the early 17th century that the handgun found use in any real number. Some clan lords - like the Date family - armed some of their mounted units with a short variant of the *teppô*, but only limited use of this weapon is recorded. This samurai wears a *tôsei gomai-dô* (*gomai* = five sections/plates) armor. The front-plate on this armor could withstand bullets from a certain distance; and many suits of armor to this day show bullet-marks sustained during testing.

# Chapter 5 - New Conquests

## WAR: AUTUMN 1551

Twice, from June 1 to July 2, Shingen pushed through to Wakamiko Castle. This was due to the troubles in Saku. But not until Ôi Danjô, the commander of Iwao Castle, surrendered on July 20 were Shingen's military plans finalized and ready to be executed. First on the agenda was the necessary tidying up in the Saku district. Shingen set off on July 30 soon reaching Sakuraiyama Castle. From there his men scoured the area for enemies.

**Photo TAK 4-12 (right)**

The hill comprising Iwao Castle in the Saku district. The river in the foreground is the Chikuma. Today it seems that parts of the castle compounds are collapsing, maybe due to the floods that from time to time occur in this area.

**Photo TAK 4-13 (below)**

Marker and a map over Iwao Castle near the entrance gate.

**Photo TAK 4-14 (below right)**

Iwao Castle's *honmaru*.

Apparently Iwao Castle was never truly occupied by the Murakami forces, but only burned to the ground. On August 28 a *kuwadate* ceremony was held at Iwao Castle while the reconstruction of Iwamurada Castle began on September 14. Oyamada Bitchû *no Kami* was installed as commander at Uchiyama, and more soldiers were assigned to these fortresses. On September 23 Shingen returned home to Tsutsujigasaki.

While Shingen was engaged with his campaign in Saku, Baba Nobuharu was following his orders to attack and capture Kariyahara Castle. Baba moved his troops north of Hirase towards Kariyahara in the Chikuma district. Baba's troops attacked the castle on August 13 and the lord of Kariyahara, Ôta Suketada, a vassal of the Ogasawara family, who had no appetite for a prolonged battle, surrendered quickly. With the capture of Kariyahara Castle, the loose ends in Chikuma

**Photo TAK 4-15 (top)**

Iwao Castle. Standing on the third compound, while looking at the second compound. The *honmaru* can be found behind the temple.

**Photo TAK 4-16 (middle)**

Another photo of the *honmaru* of Iwao Castle. Iwao Castle was built by the Ôi clan around 1478. It is a so-called low hill castle. During the Takeda invasions the castle was taken over by the Takeda and used later as a support castle for their expansions further north.

**Photo TAK 4-17 (bottom)**

One of the flanks of Iwao Castle was protected by the mighty Chikuma River. On the other side a smaller stream served as a defensive line.

were finally tied up. Shingen ordered a portion of his troops to reinforce parts of the fortifications in the area.

Just a few weeks later Murakami Yoshikiyo was once again on the move. On October 14, Murakami's army made its way towards Nyûnomi (Niugo) in the Azumi district. His target seems to have been the Nishina family, who were in support of the Takeda. Shingen learned of Yoshikiyo's movements and set off on October 15. By October 20, Shingen's army arrived at Fukashi, aiming at Hirase Castle, which lay roughly six kilometers northwest of Fukashi. Takeda controlled Hirase Castle in 1549 after Shingen's army chased Ogasawara out of Chikuma. But after Shingen's autumn 1550 defeat at Toishi his enemies recaptured Hirase. It was therefore necessary for Shingen to recapture Hirase before he could advance further north.

On October 24, his general, Hara Toratane, attacked Hirase Castle with the support of Obu and Baba. The *yamashiro* was situated on a hill 150 meters high. Its steep hillsides presented the Takeda army with a difficult task; but after two days of hard fighting (some sources state four) the lord of Hirase, Hirase Hachirôzaemon, was killed together with 204 defenders of the castle and the lord's family. In a letter to a previous Ogasawara vassal, Yamabe Sama *no Suke*, Shingen wrote that Yamabe is credited with having taken Hirase Hachirôzaemon's head.

After its capture, the castle was included in Shingen's line of base fortresses. Reconstruction of the castle began soon after the *kuwadate* ceremony was held in the main manor. On November 10, 1551 Hara Mino *no Kami* Toratane was installed as Hirase Castle's commander.

Following the castle's capture, Shingen moved his army towards Koiwadake (Koiwatake) in the Azumi district. The Koiwadake Castle lay further north. Like Hirase, it was a yamashiro, but its engineer had incorporated the mountain's natural landscape into its design. Among its natural defenses were great cliffs forming steep walls hindering any enemy attacking with a great force of men. Its commander was Koiwadake Zusho, a Murakami general.

Shingen was fully aware how difficult a task an attack of the main castle building would be, so he did not attempt a direct attack. Instead, on October 27, his troops were ordered to attack auxiliary forts in the area. Shingen's men remained in the area around the castle until November 17, when Shingen, realizing there was little possibility of a successful assault, chose to withdraw his army back to Uehara in Suwa. Lack of supplies could have also influenced his decision to withdraw.

## COLOR PLATE 1 - THE ATTACK ON INUI CASTLE (1550)

In this scene the Takeda soldiers attack a mountain fortress called Inui. The spearmen push forward, while the ashigaru units with bows fire upon the enemy. The majority of Japan's castles and fortresses were situated on mountaintops or ridgelines.

# COLOR PLATE 2 - THE ATTACK ON TOISHI CASTLE (1550)

In 1550 the Takeda army lay siege to a formidable mountain castle situated in the Chiisagata district of Shinano province. In this scene the Takeda soldiers build a defensive fence around the parts of the mountain in case the enemy tried to raid the attacker's camp. Such measures were essential in avoiding a surprise attack when nightfall came.

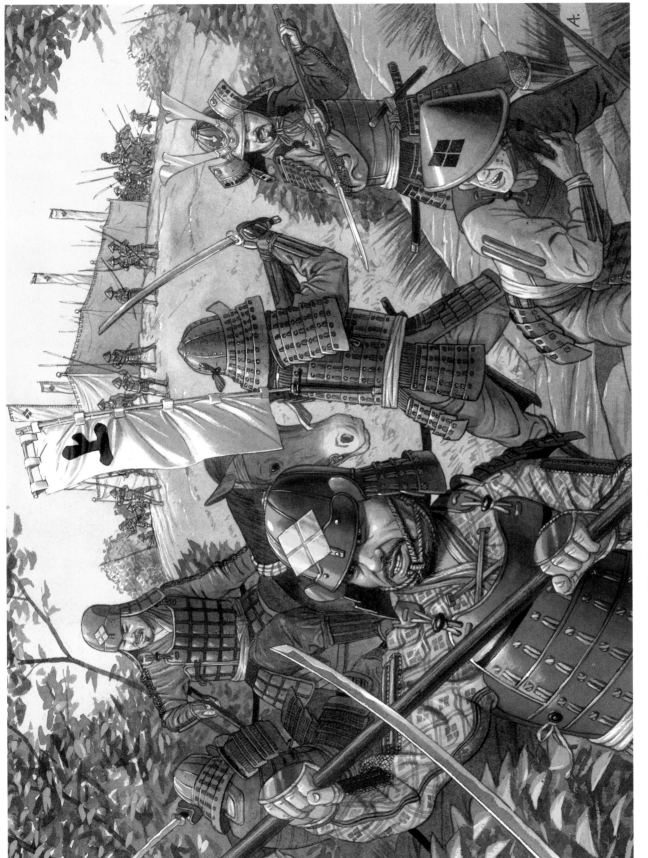

COLOR PLATE 3 - MURAKAMI ATTACKS (1550)

During the campaign against the Murakami clan the Takeda had the upper hand until a surprise attack on Shingen's honjin. Shingen's bodyguards fought desperately to hold the enemy back. They managed in the end to push the attackers away from the main camp.

# COLOR PLATE 4 – THE MAKING OF A MOUNTAIN CASTLE (1550)

During the 16th century thousands of forts and castles were built throughout Japan. Such a major undertaking utilized the farmers from nearby villages as a temporary workforce, while the samurai officers would lead the project. In order to make the fort or castle ready in time, the soldiers themselves often had to take on their share of the work. Before construction it was common to make drawings and a model of the planned castle.

## COLOR PLATE 5 - THE STANDOFF AT KAWANAKAJIMA (1553)

On five separate occasions the Uesugi and Takeda armies met on a large plain called Kawanakajima. The battle in 1553 was more a protracted standoff than an actual fight, but there was some action between the two sides. Eventually, both sides retreated without any final clash.

## COLOR PLATE 6 - THE CROSSING OF TORII PASS (1555)

During the invasion of the Kiso area in Shinano the Takeda army had to cross the 1,197 meter high mountain pass of Torii. Since some campaigns were conducted during the winter months soldiers needed solid and good clothing. Among these mountains the nights could become extremely cold, so it was imperative to keep warm. Shoes, helmets, and jackets made of straw helped a little against the cold, but were better suited to keep out the rain and snow than warm their wearers.

## COLOR PLATE 7 – THE ATTACK ON KATSURAYAMA CASTLE (1557)

The battle's climax inside Katsurayama Castle. A Takeda samurai is about to lose his head, when a comrade arrives just in the nick of time. In the background the final attack on the main keep/tower is under way.

## COLOR PLATE 8 - KAWANAKAJIMA (1557)

A Takeda division attacks the supply-train belonging to the Uesugi army. This type of attack was common during the Sengoku Period. An enemy army could not stay out in the field without supplies for very long, so a successful attack could force the majority of the enemy's army to retreat without the need for a major battle to take place.

## COLOR PLATE 9 - HONJIN (1558)

Shingen in camp, planning his army's next move. Shingen can be seen holding his distinctive helmet under his right arm. The lords in camp wear jinbaori (surcoat) over their armor. The maku curtains around the camp bear the Takeda-bishi crest.

# COLOR PLATE 10 - FUKASHI CASTLE (1560)

Fukashi Castle (later known as Matsumoto Castle) as it might have looked like during the Takeda reign. Fukashi was one of the Takeda army's main bases in Shinano province. Besides its use as a military base it served as an administrative center in the central part of Shinano.

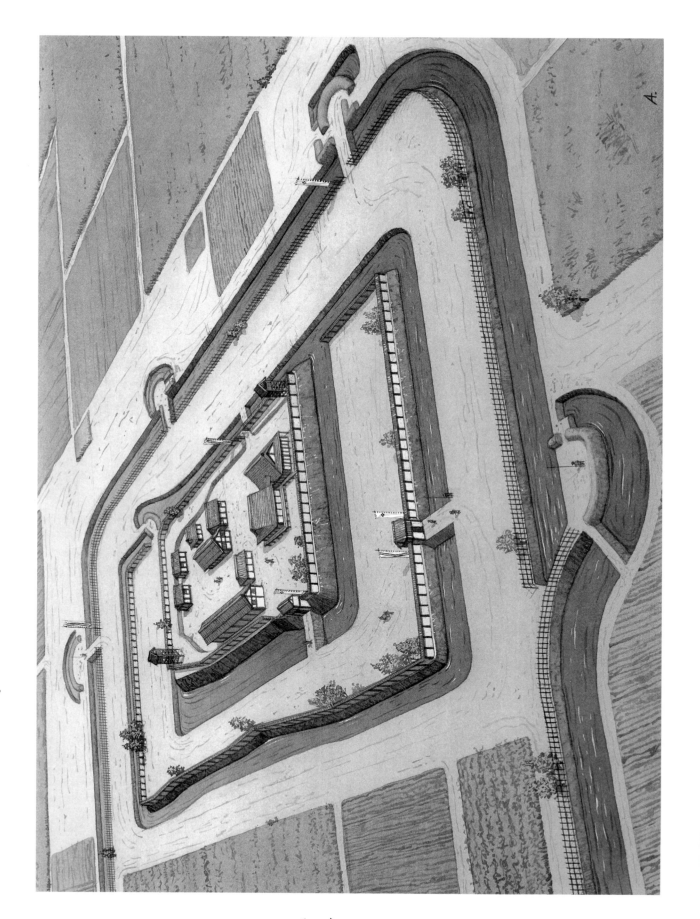

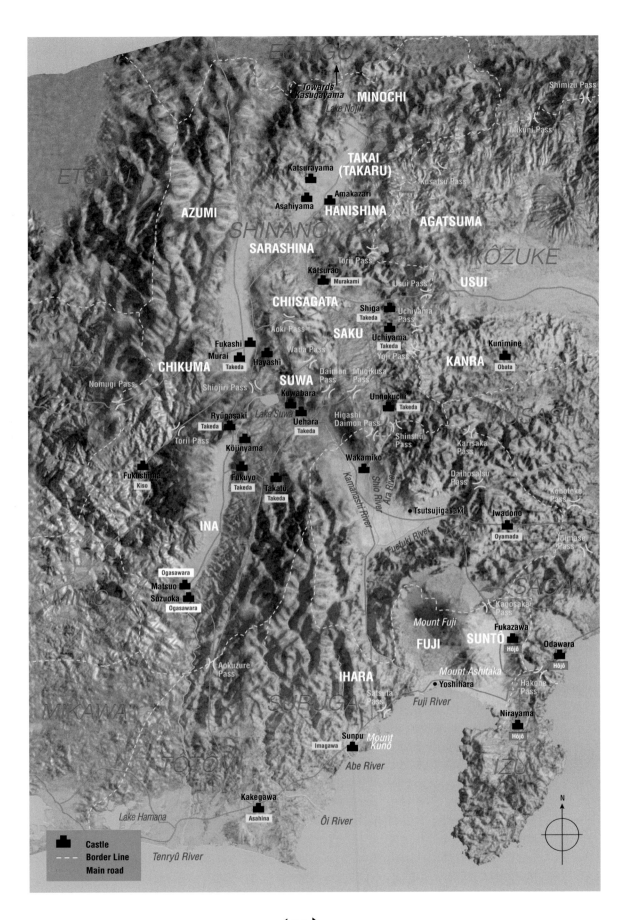

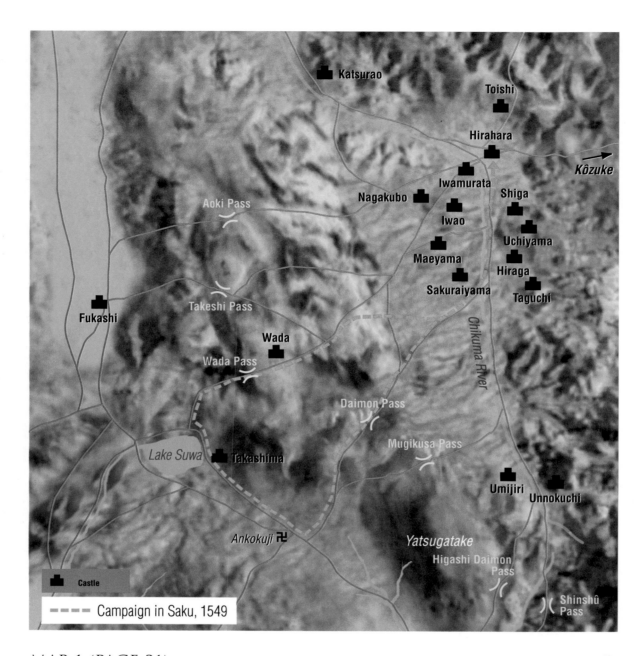

Katsurao

Toishi

Hirahara

*Kōzuke* →

Iwamurata

Nagakubo

Shiga

Iwao

Uchiyama

Maeyama

Hiraga

Sakuraiyama

Taguchi

Aoki Pass

Takeshi Pass

Fukashi

Wada

Wada Pass

Daimon Pass

Mugikusa Pass

*Chikuma River*

*Lake Suwa* Takashima

Umijiri

Unnokuchi

*Ankokuji* 卐

*Yatsugatake*

Higashi Daimon Pass

Shinshū Pass

Castle

---- Campaign in Saku, 1549

## MAP 1 (PAGE 31)

The provinces providing the stage for the Takeda during the 1550s.

## MAP 2 (ABOVE)

Campaign in Saku, 1549.

This map shows the major Takeda attack routes during their invasion of Saku in 1549.

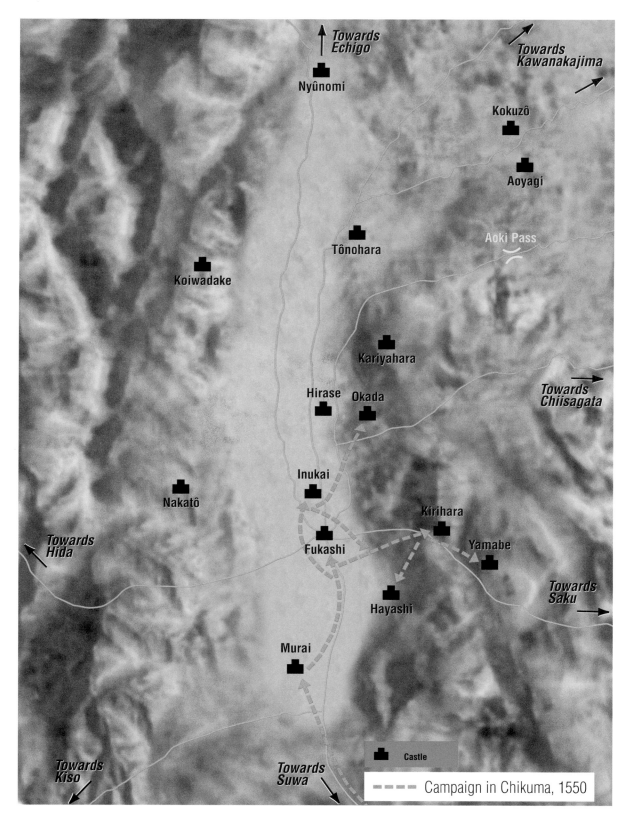

Towards
Echigo

Towards
Kawanakajima

Nyûnomi

Kokuzô

Aoyagi

Aoki Pass

Tônohara

Koiwadake

Kariyahara

Towards
Chiisagata

Hirase    Okada

Inukai

Nakatô

Kirihara

Yamabe

Towards
Hida

Fukashi

Towards
Saku

Hayashi

Murai

Castle

Towards
Kiso

Towards
Suwa

Campaign in Chikuma, 1550

MAP 3

Campaign in Chikuma, 1550.

The 1550 campaign in the Chikuma district turned into a blitzkrieg. In a few days most of the district's central area was in Takeda hands.

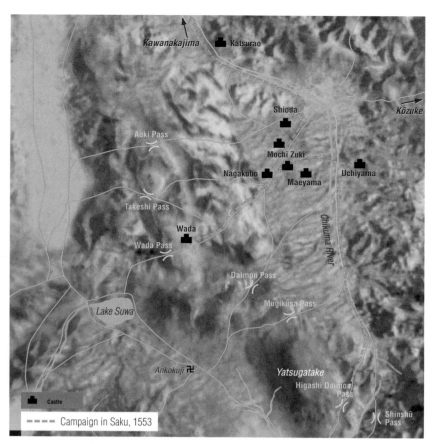

## MAP 4

Campaign in Saku, 1550.

Time and time again the Takeda were forced to invade the Saku district. The struggle with Murakami turned the Saku district into a bloody battlefield.

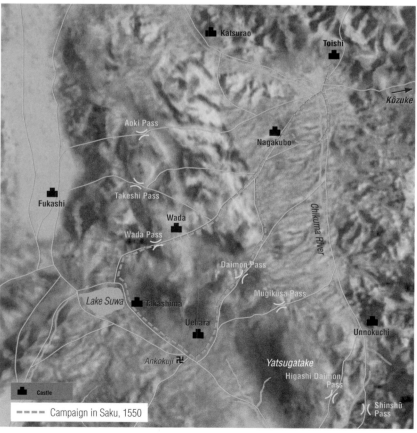

## MAP 5

Campaign in Saku, 1553.

A last attempt from Murakami to get a hold in Saku district came in 1553, but the Takeda managed to drive the hardened enemy out. Soon after, the Murakami clan's hold on this region was finally broken.

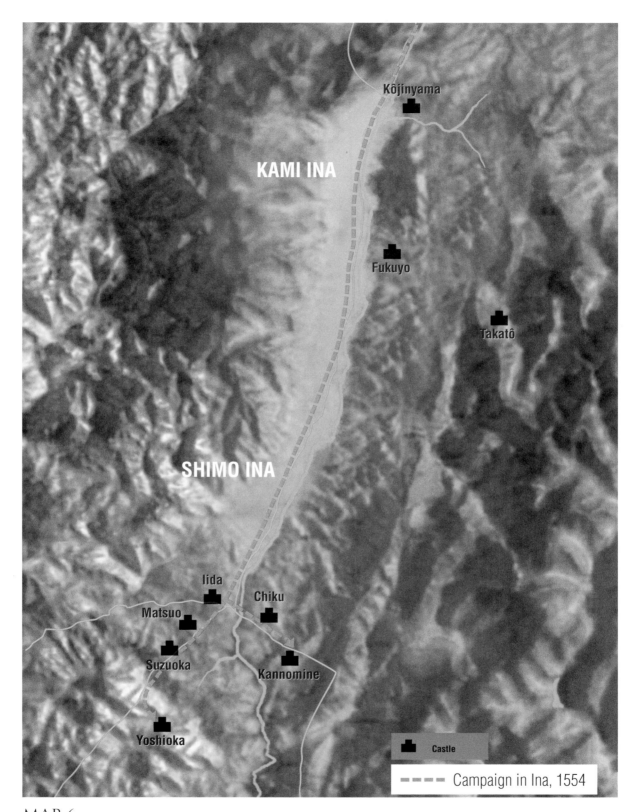

Kôjinyama

KAMI INA

Fukuyo

Takatô

SHIMO INA

Iida

Chiku

Matsuo

Suzuoka

Kannomine

Yoshioka

Castle

----- Campaign in Ina, 1554

## MAP 6

Campaign in Ina, 1554.

The northern part of Ina district had been conquered several years before; and now Shingen turned his eyes toward the southern portion. The campaign of 1554 gave the Takeda full control of the Ina district.

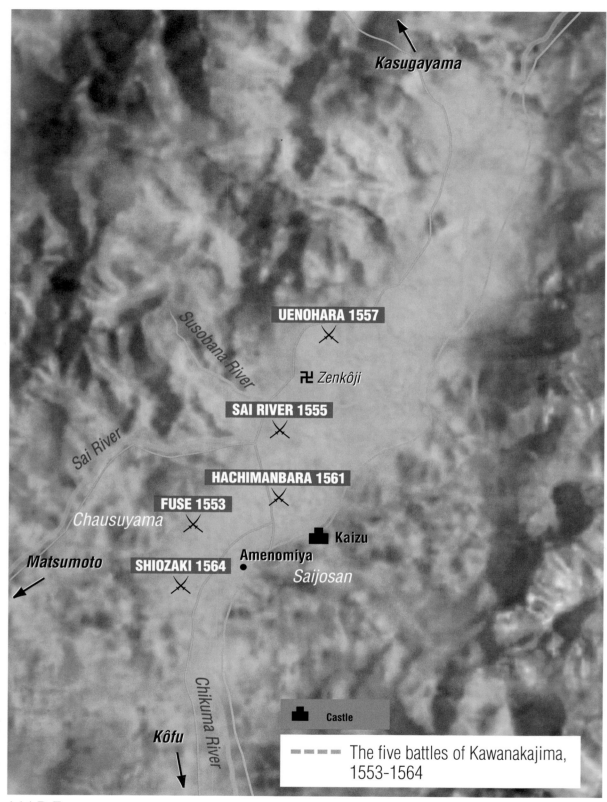

**Kasugayama**

**UENOHARA 1557**

卍 *Zenkôji*

**SAI RIVER 1555**

*Susobana River*

*Sai River*

**HACHIMANBARA 1561**

**FUSE 1553**

*Chausuyama*

🏯 **Kaizu**

**Matsumoto**

**SHIOZAKI 1564**

● **Amenomiya**

*Saijosan*

*Chikuma River*

*Kôfu*

🏯 **Castle**

- - - - - The five battles of Kawanakajima,
1553-1564

## MAP 7

The battles of Kawanakajima, 1553-1564. The map shows where the five battles of Kawanakajima took place. On five occasions the warrior houses of Takeda and Uesugi met on this large plain. The big clash in 1561 was the bloodiest of their encounters with the Takeda said to have won the day. Despite Takeda's victory, both sides suffered heavy casualties.

After a few days' rest in Suwa he traveled back to Tsutsujigasaki on November 21. Shingen spent the remainder of 1551 resting with his family at the Tsutsujigasaki Estate. The year had been an exciting one for Shingen, with most things going the Takeda clan's way. Little did he know the next year would bring further excitement.

# 1552 – THE ATTACK ON KOIWADAKE

1552 started poorly for Shingen. His faithful general of many years, Oyamada Nobuari, died on January 23, only 34 years old. It is probable he died from an illness of some sort, as there is no mention in the sources of his death on the battlefield. It was a great loss to Shingen and many others. The nearly 10,000 people attending Nobuari's burial (source: *Myôhôji-ki*) was a testament to this general's popularity.

Things were by no means quiet in the military arena either. In April, the Takeda army vanguard clashed with forces belonging to Uesugi Kenshin (Nagao Kagetora) - lord of Kasugayama in Echigo. These troops were most likely soldiers of clans from Kawanakajima who supported Kenshin. The battle was fought at Tokita. The Takeda army is said to have lost 371 men, while Uesugi's army lost only 73 men. The Takeda general, Kurihara Saemon Masakiyo, is said to have taken 17 heads on the battlefield, but received such serious injuries that he died on April 23. The Takeda army consisted of soldiers under the command of border-fortress generals in the occupied areas of Shinano, such as Hara at Hirase Castle, Baba Nobuharu at Fukashi Castle, and Sanada at Toishi Castle. It is unlikely that Shingen himself fought in the campaign. However, there is little information in the sources concerning the composition of either the Takeda or the Uesugi armies. But the source *Kôyô gunkan* claims that in the end the Takeda side was victorious, and that a battle cry of victory could be heard over much of Tokita.

In May, 1552 Shingen lost someone else who was very close to him – his mother, Ôi Fujin. Ôi Fujin was a good mother who had always supported her son. In 1541 she had chosen son instead of husband and stayed at Kai with the young Shingen when her husband, Nobutora, was sent into exile. So this loss must have affected him deeply, dampening his fighting spirit for a while, because the summer passed without new aggressions by the Takeda leader.

His period of mourning proved short lived. Having heard of the loss, Ogasawara Nagatoki calculated that Shingen would be too busy mourning to begin a military campaign. Nagatoki tried therefore to convince families in the Chikuma and Azumi districts to change their allegiance again. As these districts had previously been under the dominion of the Ogasawara family, Nagatoki knew this break in Shingen's

**Photo TAK 4-18 (top) and TAK 4-19 (above)**

Chôzenji temple where the grave of Ôi Fujin is located. Founded by the Rinzai sect of Buddhism, but exactly when is uncertain. It was first built on another site, but moved to its present location during Shingen's lifetime. Chôzenji was burned to the ground by enemy soldiers in 1582, but was rebuilt soon after.

military exploits would only provide him with so much time to make his diplomatic overtures. Some families did side once again with Nagatoki, but when Shingen received warning of this his period of mourning ended abruptly.

Shingen held a war council at Tsutsujigasaki in the late summer. Since Koiwadake Zusho, lord of Koiwadake Castle in the Azumi district, was one of the main leaders in this new rebellion Shingen and his generals decided he would be the target of an attack. This was the last fortress inside Azumi, and a victory here would give Shingen full control of the district. On the morning of July 27, the Takeda army made its way toward Shinano, and by August 1 had surrounded Kiowadake. Shingen's forces attacked at noon through a torrential rain, but by the time the rain stopped in the evening they had yet to make any gains. This first day would be one of many which would pass before the Takeda army made any progress. On the afternoon of August 12 Takeda soldiers made a violent attack on the castle, finally capturing Kiowadake. Koiwadake Zusho committed *seppuku* when he realized all hope was lost. Roughly 500 of his men were killed defending the castle. Many women and children were taken prisoner and then sold off. With this victory, the Chikuma and Azumi districts, previously under Ogasawara control, now fell under full Takeda control. The entire Matsumoto Plain now belonged to Shingen.

Shingen was satisfied with the spoils of the autumn campaign, especially the victory at Koiwadake, so no further campaigns were engaged in that year. Instead, a great feast was held on November 27 to celebrate the wedding of Shingen's son, Yoshinobu to the third daughter of Imagawa Yoshimoto. It was actually a marriage between cousins, but this was permitted in medieval Japan. As was typical for powerful families of the time, the marriage was a political one. Shingen's older sister - who had been married to Imagawa Yoshimoto – had died in 1550. With her death there were no longer any strong family bonds between the two families. These bonds were now re-established with the marriage between the son and daughter of the respective families.

**Illustration 4-11.**

*Tankô* armor, also known as *mijika-yoroi* (short armor). For approximately 700 years soldiers in Japan used this kind of armor. Used in ancient Japan during the pre-Heian period (794-1185), this armor also saw use during the early Heian period during a so-called transition period while the newer Ô-*yoroi* armor came into production. It was mainly metal, but also contained pieces of leather and bark. This armor served mainly to protect the chest and back, but with the inclusion of the helmet it was a relatively good suit of protective armor. It also came with a *kusazuri* skirt, similar to the one seen on the *keikô* armor.

# Chapter 6 - The Dreaded Enemy: Uesugi Kenshin

## COUNTDOWN TO KAWANAKAJIMA

In January 1553 Shingen was faced with a threat from the north. In 1550, Ogasawara Nagatoki had fled north to Shinano, where he thought he could enlist the help of Uesugi Kenshin. Kenshin was a powerful lord from Echigo, and like Shingen, Kenshin was also hungry for land. This voracious appetite ensured that he and Shingen would clash sooner or later. In April 1552, troops from the two families had sparred at Tokita, but this was a small taste of what was to come.

**Photo TAK 4-20**

Uesugi Kenshin (1530-1578). Kenshin was one of Shingen's most hardened opponents and met the Takeda general at Kawanakajima five times without any final decision. Neither could truly claim victory, but both of them did. (Isawa *onsen* festival in Kôfu).

Before Shingen could advance against Uesugi Kenshin in the Kawanakajima region, which was the northern part of the Shinano province, he had first to defeat Murakami Yoshikiyo at Katsurao Castle. Two roads led to Kawanakajima. The first road passed through Matsumoto in Chikuma before turning east towards the Sarashina district. The Matsumoto area had been under the Ogasawara family's control, but was now completely under Takeda control, giving Shingen the ability to move against Kawanakajima from that direction. The second road connected the Saku district and Hanishina where Murakami governed. Shingen could choose the road through Matsumoto, but he risked being attacked from the rear by Murakami when he emerged onto the Kawanakajima Plain. Therefore, if Shingen was going to advance further north in Shinano it was imperative that Katsurao Castle be captured first and Murakami's head taken. Murakami Yoshikiyo had humbled Shingen on the battlefield on two separate occasions and the time for revenge had come. Shingen now concentrated all his strength on this task.

On January 28, Shingen sent a messenger with a letter to his general, Oyamada Masatatsu, at Uchiyama Castle in Saku. The letter informed Oyamada that Shingen would be arriving at Saku around February 6, and he should prepare himself for Shingen's visit. The plan was ostensibly to hold a ceremony at Toishi Castle, perhaps a *kuwadate* ceremony. However, what was really happening was an attempt to trick Murakami at Katsurao into believing that something as innocent as a ceremony would be held inside Toishi. Apparently, Shingen also included his host, Oyamada, in this deception. Perhaps Shingen felt that not revealing the truth behind his plan would increase his chances of success. We must not forget either that *shinobi* were moving in the shadows at all times. So to spread disinformation to as many people as possible was no doubt a wise move. This was one of his first steps in bringing about the final defeat of his archenemy, Murakami Yoshikiyo.

Shingen set off on March 23, after all preparations had been made, but not towards Saku. Shingen's army passed Uehara Castle in Suwa, approaching instead the Shiojiri Pass, whereupon he entered Fukashi Castle on March 30. However, this date may be wrong, because in the source *Kôhakusai-ki* it is noted that Shingen set off from Fukashi Castle on March 29. From Fukashi the army advanced north, making camp near Kariyahara Castle - northeast of Fukashi. Shingen's plan was to advance through the Matsumoto area and then swing around to the northwest side of Katsurao - in other words to approach Katsurao from the unexpected north side in the hope that this surprise move would catch his enemy off guard and improve his chances of taking the castle easily. This bold plan would also isolate Katsurao, thereby bringing Murakami down without the use of force.

The next day Shingen's troops set fire to the villages in the area, and on March 30 the army stormed Kariyahara Castle. The castle defenders fought valiantly, raining showers of arrows down on the sieging forces, but the Takeda troops used shields of bamboo to defend themselves from the deadly rainstorm as they made an attacking raid up the mountainside. Although Kariyahara was only a small mountain fortress, the defenders fought to the bitter end. The castle proved to be more difficult for Takeda to capture than had been expected, but on April 2 the castle was finally stormed and taken.

Some of the sources concerning Kariyahara Castle contradict each other. It was noted earlier that Baba Nobuharu had captured it in August 1551. This provides us then with two possibilities: the castle was not captured in August 1551; or it was captured, but the lord changed sides when the Takeda army withdrew, and was now recaptured by Shingen.

The most likely story, then, is that Kariyahara Castle was stormed and razed in 1553, and the castle's lord, Ôta Nagato *no Kami*, was taken prisoner. On April 8 Imafuku Iwami *no Kami* was appointed commander of what was to be the new Kariyahara Castle and a *kuwadate* ceremony was held inside the main compound.

North of Kariyahara lay Tônohara Castle. This fortress was taken on April 2; this time without a clash of arms. The next day the Takeda army pillaged the areas near Aida and to the east of Aida, at the foot of the Kokûzô Mountain. When the defenders at Kokûzô Fort learned the Takeda army was storming their direction they fled as fast as their feet could carry them. None wished to die at the end of a Takeda sword or arrow. The fort was burned just like so many others had been. From Fukashi and all the way up to Katsurao fortresses and villages were stormed and then secured by Takeda's vanguard troops; this ensured Shingen and his main force would not be ambushed. The *shinobi*, also known as *ninja*, were a constant threat to officers of high rank in the field. These shadowy assassins could strike at any moment, making searching and securing areas ahead of an army's advance a top priority.

On April 6, Shingen dispatched a vanguard force led by twelve of his generals with orders to surround Katsurao Castle, which they soon did. At this time several of the Murakami clan's allies went over to Shingen, including the Yashiro, Shiozaki, Ishikawa, Obinata (Ôbinata), and Ôsuga families. This weakened Yoshikiyo's possibilities considerably leaving him nearly alone in his fight against Shingen.

It is clear that Yoshikiyo realized the battle was lost before it had begun. When Shingen's generals arrived on the morning of April 9 the castle gates were opened, but Yoshikiyo was nowhere to be seen. Clearly, the Takeda army's iron ring around the castle was not as secure as thought, and Yoshikiyo had once again managed to escape, making his way north to Uesugi Kenshin in Echigo. On April 12, Takeda Nobushige and Komai Masatake took over Katsurao Castle. The main reason for Shingen's victory over Murakami this time was probably that after their castles and forts were captured he managed to get the *fudai* families (inner circle) in the area to break their alliance with Yoshikiyo. This left Yoshikiyo isolated, unable to stand against such an eager enemy with the few men at his disposition.

**Photo TAK 4-21**

A board telling the story of Katsurao Castle, with a map of the various compounds of the castle as well. It can be found near the entrance path to the castle.

**Photo TAK 4-22**

The opposite side of Chikuma River, seen from Katsurao Castle. Katsurao lay between Sakaki and Yashiro where the southern edge of Kawanakajima begins, making it a very important castle to control.

**Photo TAK 4-23**

Evidence of stone used in the castle's foundations can be seen at several places at Katsurao Castle.

**Photo TAK 4-24**

Photo taken from the northern side of Katsurao and Hime Castles. Hime Castle lay at the tip of the ridge, to the right, with Katsurao further up to the left. The Chikuma River flows below.

**Photo TAK 4-25 (above) & TAK4-26 (above right)**

Two photos of the *honmaru* of Katsurao Castle. The castle was built by the Murakami family, but exactly when is unclear. Historians believe it was constructed sometime during the end of the 14th century. It was held by the Murakami clan until the Takeda armies captured it in 1553.

**Photo TAK 4-27**

Another photo taken from the northern side of Katsurao and Hime Castles. Hime Castle lay at the tip of the ridge, to the right, with Katsurao further up to the left. The Chikuma River flows below.

**Photo TAK 4-28**

The mountains where Katsurao and Hime Castles are located, looking from the mountains above Wago Castle, which lay between the Ueda and Sakaki areas. The Sakaki area was ruled by the Murakami family. The Chikuma River runs along the foot of Hime Castle, making a sharp turn at the base.

Shingen received the news that Katsurao Castle had been taken; and on April 15 he set off for Kariyahara, his army advancing northwards before making camp at Aoyagi. On April 16 a messenger arrived at Shingen's *honjin* with a letter from the Kôsaka family. The Kôsaka family hailed from the southern end of the Kawanakajima Plain in the Sarashina district; and were declaring their support of Shingen. The next day a *kuwadate* ceremony was held inside the Aoyagi fortress where Shingen also appointed Oso Genpachi to govern Katsurao. Oso had a force of roughly 300 men, a small force with which to defend the vulnerable northern front line. It was not long before his men were put to the test.

While Shingen was consolidating his newly acquired land, Yoshikiyo, who had not given up the fight against Takeda,

had managed to gain the support of Uesugi Kenshin, the most powerful lord in the north. Uesugi Kenshin was well aware of the problems in Shinano, because several small families from the northern part of Shinano (including Ogasawara Nagatoki) had also contacted him for help. From this moment on Kenshin took a direct hand in the conflicts in Shinano.

Yoshikiyo acted quickly, his army advancing along the banks of the Chikuma River on the Kawanakajima plain on April 22 (another source states June). The army numbered roughly 5,000 men (another source states 10,000). Part of the army came from Echigo and included soldiers from the families in northern Shinano. Yoshikiyo also had the support of other families, such as the Shimazu, and Inoue, but whether or not Kenshin participated in person is uncertain. Some of the sources indicate Takanashi Masayori also took part. There is some doubt concerning who actually took part on Murakami's side, because the sources give conflicting accounts. Yoshikiyo was hoping to recapture Katsurao then drive the Takeda army out of the Sarashina district.

Shingen's camp lay at the foot of the Ubasute (Obasute) Mountain, not far from the Hachiman temple, with vanguard divisions further out on Kawanakajima at a place called Zenkôji Plain. Takeda's vanguard forces soon clashed with the Echigo army, but withdrew rapidly. The Murakami/ Uesugi army now pushed further towards Katsurao. The army surrounded Katsurao and the castle was stormed on April 23. Oso Genpachi fought bravely, but fell in the battle together with his men. Takeda Shingen knew the disposition of both armies favored an enemy victory at this point, and on April 24 withdrew his troops to Kariyahara. On May 1 he entered Fukashi Castle, and once the army had gathered set off for Kai. On May 11 the army was back at Tsutsujigasaki.

## KAWANAKAJIMA 1553

Yoshikiyo had recaptured Katsurao, but the castle was not put to serious use, because he did not think it strong enough to defend itself against the Takeda army. Instead, Yoshikiyo used Shioda castle, southwest of Katsurao, as his new base. He anticipated another attack by Shingen soon, so he decided to mobilize, but did not manage to enlist enough soldiers. He hoped his old allies and vassals would flock to join him, unfortunately only 2,000 soldiers turned up, as many stayed loyal to the Takeda, or decided to avoid problems with the Takeda. The coalition army had also managed to take a handful of fortresses from Katsurao to Wada before the battles were over. These defenses would aid Murakami when Shingen returned, but he still lacked troops.

Shingen was not chased from the area after the defeat at Katsurao, but instead left by his own choosing. A new

**Photo TAK 4-29 (top)**

The *Tora-guchi* gate at Shioda Castle. This is also the compound where the well was located.

**Photo TAK 4-30 (above)**

Shioda Castle lay among these mountains. Not what might be expected, as most castles were built on the tops of mountains. Shioda Castle differs from other castles in the 16$^{th}$ century, this due to the fact that it goes back to the 13$^{th}$ century, and was originally a mansion. It was built by Hôjô Yoshimasa, and for generations it served as their base in Shioda. During the Sengoku Period it was under the Murakami clan's control, but was lost to the Takeda in the 1550s.

variable in the fray, Uesugi Kenshin was a powerful lord, someone Shingen wanted to be better prepared for before commiting to an all out war. He used the summer to make plans for the coming autumn campaign. Kenshin had in no way entered into this war involuntarily. He was fully aware of Shingen's ambitions, and knew if the Kawanakajima families were crushed he himself could be the next target. It was therefore absolutely necessary for Kenshin to make allies with the families in the northern part of Shinano who still stood against the Takeda clan. This time the great difference for Shingen was that he and his opponent were cut from the same cloth, both in ambition and in military ability. Both could muster large military forces, so the entire affair would most likely be decided on a strategic level, with ample help from their *shinobi*.

Shingen set off for the Saku district from Tsutsujigasaki on July 25, taking with him roughly 5,000 soldiers. The army marched in to Saku, camping at Uchiyama Castle on July 28, before heading northeast and making camp at Mochizuki on the 30. The following day, his troops advanced further to the west, towards the Wada Pass, camping near Nagakubo in the Chiisagata district on August 1. It was here Shingen attacked his first target, Wada Castle. The castle represented the front line of the Echigo and Shinano armies. It was stormed and its defenders killed; on August 4, Takatoya Castle suffered the same fate. Later the same day, Shingen's army marched down to the Uchimura River where they stormed Uchimura Castle that evening. With the way clear, the army advanced on Shioda on the morning of August 5. Once in position, the army stormed and seized the castle. Nobody knew where Yoshikiyo was: once again he had deserted a sinking ship like a rat. According to the source *Myôhôji-ki*, sixteen other fortresses were taken in the course of one day, and many so-called *ashiyowa* were taken prisoner. Shingen made short work of taming Shioda Castle, and appointed his general, Obu Toramasa, as commander. With this victory against Murakami Yoshikiyo the Chiisagata district was yet again under Takeda control.

After the tidying up in Chiisagata, Shingen ordered his men to advance towards Kawanakajima, by the middle of August the army arrived at Fuse, which lies in the southern part of Kawanakajima. No one quite knew where Murakami Yoshikiyo was or what had happened to him, but he had most likely sought refuge north in Shinano, where he could have made contact with Uesugi and once again requested aid. This possibility was borne out as an Uesugi army of roughly 8,000 soon marched south on the Kawanakajima Plain. In reality, the Uesugi army was a coalition army comprised of soldiers from families including the Murakami, Takanashi, Inoue, Shimazu, Suda, and Kurita families. As far as the military action between the two clans is concerned, there was no decisive battle, but instead a series of small clashes over a wide expanse of territory. The encounters began in early September and lasted until September 17. The forces clashed in both the Chikuma and Hanishina districts, with several fortresses stormed and villages burned. There was also a clash near Hachiman (Yawata), which Uesugi won, and another battle is said to have taken place on September 15 near Fuse.

The clashes between the two sides ended when Uesugi Kenshin withdrew his soldiers on September 20. Shingen chose to stay in the area because troops from other families remained to cause havoc. Once these families were under control there was no longer any looming danger, and on October 7 Shingen finally withdrew his army to Fukashi Castle. After a short rest at Fukashi the army moved on,

**Photo TAK 4-31**

Fuse area, near the bridge over the river. It was in this area that the Takeda and Uesugi had their first battle of Kawanakajima. The ridge to the left, on the highest hill, is Yashiro Castle.

reaching Kai by October 17. Kenshin is said to have withdrawn because of a planned journey to the capital, Kyôto. Because no decisive battle was fought with his opponent, Kenshin had simply run out of time and had other obligations to meet. This battle was the first of the famous battles at Kawanakajima. It ended without any decisive victor, but Shingen was the last to leave the battlefield, which may be counted as a point in Takeda's favor. After Uesugi left, the families in the northern part of Shinano stood completely alone, offering Shingen the possibility of tightening his grip. The Chiisagata district, which had recently changed owners, was divided between Shingen's vassals, who built new fortresses reconstructing and reinforcing others.

Winter now came to the mountains in Kai and Shinano, naturally putting a damper on military campaigns. Shingen and his family therefore shared a peaceful period towards the end of the year.

**Illustration 4-12.**

This suit of armor is known as Ô-yoroi (big armor). This kind of armor replaced the *tankô* and *keikô* armors during the Heian period (794-1185). It is also referred to as a box-armor. It consisted for the most part of metal and leather laced together with colorful threads. This kind of armor belonged to cavalry warriors – the samurai. For centuries this was their uniform. By this time, leg protectors made of metal and leather had come into use. He wears a *tachi* sword, a *tantô* (dagger), and carries a *yumi* and an *ebira* (a certain kind of quiver).

# Chapter 7 – War and Alliance in the South

## THE BATTLE OF KARIYA RIVER - 1554

1554 appeared as though it would start quite peacefully, but in the middle of the snowy winter Yoshimoto from Suruga knocked on the door. In February, Yoshimoto invaded the territories of Kira Yoshiyasu in the Mikawa province. Imagawa Yoshimoto's nearest neighbor, Mikawa, lay to the west of the Suruga and Tôtômi provinces. This attack was not an impetuous attack, but was a long time in its planning. The attack against the Kira family gave Hôjô Ujiyasu in Sagami an opportunity to try to exploit the situation. He marched over the border with a large army and the Hôjô soldiers flowed into the Imagawa family's territories. This resulted in a critical situation for Yoshimoto, because he had his hands full in Mikawa, and for a while he was at a loss for what to do. He solved the problem by sending a messenger to Shingen in Kai asking for the Takeda's assistance in defending Suruga. Since the two families were allies, Shingen was obliged to help out.

Taking personal command of the force making its way to Suruga, Shingen marched along the banks of the Fuji River towards Mansawaguchi. Hôjô Ujiyasu advanced further towards the west throwing the entire area below Mount Fuji into turmoil. Ujiyasu was unaware the Takeda army was on the march, so without giving a thought to a possible enemy from the north, his army made camp at Yoshihara and Kashiwahara, areas inside the Fuji district. Shingen and his men crossed the border into Suruga and made camp at Yanagijima not far from Fuji town. Although the Imagawa soldiers were also on the march whether or not they took part in the decisive battle that followed is a mystery.

The battle was fought near the Kariya River on March 3, 1554, with the Fuji Mountain forming a backdrop. The sources point to Takeda as the victor, but Shingen's army is also said to have suffered heavy losses. Imagawa Yoshimoto's forces, which were returning from Mikawa, are also reputed to have clashed with the Hôjô army.

However, there are no references to the battle in the contemporary histories of the Hôjô, Imagawa, or Takeda, the three parties involved. On the basis of this, some historians believe that the whole episode from March 1554 was concocted at a later date. If that is the case, then what was Shingen doing in the period February/March 1554, if not in Suruga fighting Hôjô? The author has been unable to answer this question, but without other references to challenge the episode in Suruga; it is possible that the battle did actually take place.

# 1554 - THE ALLIANCE

The war in Suruga ended in a peace agreement between the three families involved in the summer of 1554 – this agreement is known as *Zentokuji no kaimei*. The architect behind the alliance was Imagawa Yoshimoto's main strategist, Taigen Sessai, a priest from the Rinzai temple (Rinzai is a sect of Buddhism). The parties involved are said to have met each other at the Zentokuji temple in Suruga.

However, whether they actually met at Zentokuji or whether the whole thing was accomplished through messengers is unclear, because the sources diverge on this point as well. Sessai is said to have proposed marriage between the various families in order to seal the agreement. The hand of Shingen's daughter was promised in marriage to Hôjô Ujiyasu's son, Ujimasa, and Ujiyasu's daughter was engaged to Yoshimoto's son, Ujizane. Shingen's son, Yoshinobu, was already married to Yoshimoto's daughter. These marriages bound the three families together, establishing a basis for future peaceful cooperation. Sources such as *Kôyô gunkan, Hôjô-ki, Hôjô godai-ki,* and *Sôshû heiran-ki* support the above scenario.

Speculation exists that the alliance was formed because the three had common interests, or rather enemies. Takeda and Hôjô had gradually advanced further north, Shingen in Shinano and Hôjô in Kôzuke, and were now faced with common enemies in the north, among them the Uesugi clan. Imagawa Yoshimoto was the only one to advance west along the coast, but the alliance suited him well as he needed to guard his rear.

Once again, sources differ, with some historians theorizing the agreement between Takeda and Hôjô was made before the conflict in Suruga erupted. In support of this theory, they refer to the source *Kôhakusai-ki,* which states that two members of the Takeda and Hôjô families were engaged to be married in 1553. On January 17, 1554, a messenger from Odawara (the Hôjô clan) arrived in Kôfu with a letter containing a promise of loyalty from Ujiyasu. On February 21, Shingen answered with a similar letter to Hôjô in Odawara. In the source *Myôhôji-ki* we find the following: in February 1554 an engagement was entered into between Shingen's daughter and Hôjô Ujiyasu's son, Ujimasa. It further states that in July 1554 a wedding was held between Hôjô Ujiyasu's daughter and Yoshimoto's son, Imagawa Ujizane.

According to these two sources, then, it was not Sessai who arranged the alliance at Zentokuji temple in the summer of 1554. Some historians believe that the entire story relating to Sessai is pure fiction, concocted during the Edo period (1603-1867). But these sources do suggest that an agreement was made between the Imagawa and Hôjô families in the summer of 1554.

The wedding between Takeda Shingen's daughter and Hôjô Ujimasa is said to have taken place during December 1554. The bride was given away at Uenohara in the Tsuru district in Kai. Hôjô Ujiyasu's daughter was given away at Mishima in Suruga in July.

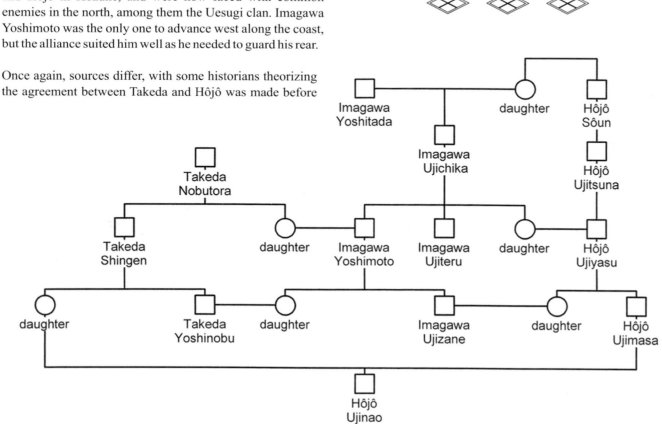

# Chapter 8 - Southern Shinano

## INVASION OF SHIMO INA

**B**y the late summer of 1554, everything was ready for the planned autumn campaign. Shingen had targeted the southern part of Ina called the Shimo Ina (Shimo means 'lower') district of Shinano. Since the capture of the northern part of Ina (Kami Ina; Kami means 'upper') in 1545, the families in the south had been left in peace. As already mentioned, Shingen had given priority to the north of Shinano, but now he was ready to invade and conquer the rest of Ina.

On July 24 the army once again marched from Kôfu. The vanguard troops of 3,000 cavalry set course into the northern part of the Ina district. Understandably, the families in Shimo Ina became quite uneasy when they heard of these new developments. Shingen planned to attack and capture a number of fortresses, including Suzuoka in Matsuo, where Ogasawara Nobusada (younger brother of Ogasawara Nagatoki) was in command; Kannomine (Jinnomine), where Chiku Yorimoto was in command; and Yoshioka, where the Shimojô family resided. The first fortress to be attacked was Suzuoka on August 7, quickly sending Nobusada into full flight to the south. At first he placed his trust in the Shimojô family, but he soon fled further and ended up as a *rônin* (a samurai without a master), wandering around the Suruga and Ise provinces.

Many of the smaller clans in the area now chose to surrender without a fight, pledging their loyalty to Takeda, most likely because they were scared of losing everything they had managed to gain over the years. However, despite the poor odds there were some who chose to fight and would have to be persuaded to surrender to the Takeda the hard way. Under the command of Yamagata Masakage, the Takeda army attacked Chiku Yorimoto's fortress, Kannomine. Yorimoto and his men put up a desperate defense, but despite this large parts of the area were put to the torch. Many temples were also burned down with no mercy shown to any men bearing arms against Takeda. The superior Takeda forces proved to be too strong for this type of scattered resistance, and in the end the defenders of Kannomine surrendered. Yorimoto, his son, Yoshirô, and six other generals were taken prisoner and sent to Kai, or more specifically Unoshima on Lake Kawaguchi. Here they were imprisoned, but on May 28, 1555, at Funatsu, not far from the lake, they were all executed - forced to commit *seppuku*. This above information comes from the source *Myôhôji-ki*, but the source *Kôyô gunkan* tells another story: the Chiku family faithfully served the Takeda until 1582, from then on they served the Tokugawa, or more correctly it was Chiku Yoriuji and his 15 cavalry who took service with the Tokugawa. So, according to this source it was not Yorimoto and his son Yoshirô that were killed at Funatsu in Tsuru district in Kai. Another source states that Chiku Yorimoto surrendered to the Takeda in 1552, becoming a Takeda vassal.

When Shimojô Nobuuji, the commander of Yoshioka fortress, heard of the havoc caused by the Takeda army he completely lost his will to fight, choosing instead to pledge his loyalty to Shingen. He had now captured the southern part of Ina, claiming it for the Takeda clan. Shingen appointed his general, Akiyama Nobutomo, to administer the Ina district using Takatô Castle as his base. On August 26, the Takeda army set course for the Kiso-guchi area in the Chikuma district, northwest of Kami Ina. The first family forced into submission was the Mimura family. According to the *Kôyô gunkan*, at the end of September Mimura and 213 members of his clan were executed near the Ichirenji temple in Kôfu.

The Takeda army is said to have invaded the western part of the Chikuma district, with some sources detailing a battle was fought near Fukushima Castle in the late autumn of 1554. In this battle between Kiso Yoshiyasu (1514-1579) and Takeda Shingen, Shingen was the victor. Despite this source's information, the majority of sources specify the date of August 1555 as the time when the Kiso clan became vassals after their defeat. It is also possible, though, that a battle was fought which Shingen did not win outright, and that the Kiso family continued to govern over their own territories for one more year.

## REBELLION IN SAKU

While Shingen focused his efforts on the southern part of Ina, a rebellion broke out in the Saku district. This was most likely a festering resentment to the outcome at Kawanakajima the year before. Shingen sent his sixteen-year-old son, Yoshinobu on his first campaign to crush the rebellion. Although Yoshinobu had taken part in the campaign in Shimo Ina, Shingen thought this would present his son with a real challenge. Yoshinobu and his generals set off for Saku, attacking nine forts in the course of one afternoon. Komoro Castle surrendered without a battle, and together with the soldiers from Uchiyama Castle the Takeda army continued its advance. In all 300 heads were taken.

**Photo TAK 4-32 (top)** The third gate of Komoro Castle. Komoro appears today as it did at the end of the Sengoku Period, when it was controlled by the Sengoku clan. Exactly what it looked like during the Takeda era is unclear. Not much information remains and the new castle was most likely built on top of the old ruins, making it difficult to estimate the size and shape of the old castle.

**Photo TAK 4-33 (second)** Standing near the entrance to the second compound of Komoro Castle.

**Photo TAK 4-34 (third)** Standing in front of the Kuromon Bridge leading onto the *honmaru* and *umagoya* compound of Komoro Castle.

**Photo TAK 4-35 (bottom)** Standing on the ruins of the main keep, looking down on the ruins of what would have been the *umagoya* compound (the horse stable compound) of Komoro Castle. The Ôi family first constructed the castle in 1487. Later in 1543 it was taken over by the Takeda, and under the supervision of Baba Nobufusa it underwent a major reconstruction. After the collapse of the Takeda clan in 1582, it was taken over by Yoda Nobushige (1548-1583), but soon after his son, Yoda (Matsudaira) Yasukuni (1570-1590) took over. After 1590 the castle went over to the Sengoku family.

# Chapter 9 – Political Games in Shinano

## POLITICAL STRATEGY

**A**fter the conquest of the Ina district and quelling the rebellion in Saku, Shingen was now ready for new challenges, and spent the winter of 1554 plotting intrigues in Shinano. Shingen realized that Uesugi Kenshin was a powerful enemy, one who would undoubtedly be his most difficult opponent north in Shinano. Kenshin had his base in Echigo, but like Shingen he was also interested in the province. Kenshin knew the benefits in maintaining Shinano as a buffer between his territories and those of the Takeda and if Shinano fell to Shingen's mighty army, then Echigo could well be his next goal. Uesugi therefore followed a strategy of intensive alliance-making in both Shinano and Echigo. Like Shingen, though, Kenshin also used military power when diplomacy did not achieve its goals, so Shingen's plan was now to break up the network of alliances Kenshin had carefully constructed.

**Illustration 4-13.**

A *keikô* armor. The differences between the *keikô* and *tankô* armors are quite easy to spot. Chinese influences are apparent, and it apparently made its appearance in Japan during the 5^th century. Protecting the whole upper body and thighs made it a solid suit of armor. It consisted of roughly 800 metal plates laced together. The skirt protected the thigh area of the wearer, and this construction and development continued in Japan, leading later to the four *kusazuri* plates on the Ô-yoroi armor. This soldier wears a *mabisashi tsuki kabuto* on his head.

In September, Shingen sent Amari Masatada (1533-1564?) to Kitajô Takahiro, the lord of Kitajô Castle, in the Kariwa district in Echigo urging Takahiro to rebel against Uesugi. Shingen most likely promised Kitajô help if he rebelled, because without support Kitajô stood no chance of surviving any invasion. Amari Masatada was successful in his mission and Takahiro raised the flag of rebellion. Before long, Uesugi Kenshin reacted to this insurgency and stormed Kitajô Castle in February 1555. No help from Shingen arrived, and Takahiro, realizing the battle was lost, surrendered. Nevertheless, he managed to keep his head on his shoulders, was even forgiven for his actions, and once again entered the service of Uesugi. Why Shingen didn't help Kitajô is not known, but it is possible he was occupied elsewhere. It also involved a great risk to advance into Echigo without more support in the area. Kenshin had also reacted very quickly to the rebellion, and perhaps this was a ploy by Shingen to gauge his foe's ability to quickly react to rebellions.

However, Shingen did not abandon his alliance-breaking strategy, and decided to focus his efforts on families in the Azumi and Minochi districts in Shinano. These areas bordered Echigo where several of the families in the area were allied with Uesugi. Shingen ordered troops into these districts and families there were pressured into changing sides, even storming Senmi Castle in the Azumi district.

**Illustration 4-14.**

A suit of *dô-maru* armor. This armor was used throughout the Japanese Middle Ages. It seems to have made its appearance during the middle of the Heian period (794-1185) and is believed to be a transition from the *keikô* style of armor. The *dô-maru's* popularity lasted throughout the Sengoku period. Like the *Ô-yoroi* armor, it was made up of metal and leather laced together with colorful threads. Hundreds of different types of *dô-maru* armor existed, with each clan or owner adding their own unique flare to the suit. While the samurai on horseback used the *Ô-yoroi*, the foot soldier, both foot samurai and low ranking soldiers, used *dô-maru* armor. The soldier illustrated is well-armed with a *naginata*, a *tachi*, and a *tantô*.

**Illustration 4-15.**

*Haramaki* armor. Along with the *dô-maru* this was another suit of armor making its appearance during the Heian period. Its main difference from the *dô-maru* was the opening at the back while the *dô-maru's* opening was under the right arm. If a soldier could afford a more expensive suit of armor, he or she could attach an extra plate to cover the gap at the back. This samurai holds a *kama-yari* in his right hand; attached to the belt is a *tachi* sword.

# Chapter 10 – The Kiso Clan

## INVASION OF KISO

In mid-January 1555, the Takeda army marched through the Torii Pass in the Chikuma district. The target of this campaign was the Kiso family's Fukushima Castle. Winter in this region was not the best time of the year to set off on a military campaign. Not only did the biting cold cut through the soldiers' uniforms, but heavy snows made even normal travel a nightmare. Fukushima was a strong mountain castle, and the Takeda troops were easily held at bay by its defenders. After five days of fighting the Takeda army gave up and withdrew to Fukashi. It could be surmised that Shingen's forces were delayed in their return from the aborted siege at Fukushima and were unable to reach Kitajô in time to help defend him from Kenshin as he had promised.

**Photo TAK 4-36**

The Kiso Fukushima valley in Kiso. The valley was governed over by the Kiso clan for centuries until the Takeda forced the Kiso clan to become Takeda vassals in the 1550s. Photo taken from the road leading up to the Fukushima Castle.

On two previous occasions Shingen had ground to a dead stop in his efforts to capture the Kiso clan's Fukushima Castle, but he had by no means given up. A large force was mobilized and ordered to march again towards the Torii Pass, arriving there on March 18. At the passage into the Kiso Valley the Takeda soldiers built a temporary fortress which overlooked the Yabuhara Plain. At the fortress Shingen divided his force into two divisions. One of the divisions, under the command of Hara Masatane, attacked towards the River Na, and then advanced further towards Yabuhara. Here Hara's division clashed with some of Kiso Yoshiyasu's troops, but Hara's men were unstoppable, quickly routing Yoshiyasu's troops. While Shingen's men were engaged in the campaign against Kiso information reached him around April 3 via his *tsukaiban* (messenger) that Kenshin was making his way to Kawanakajima. He chose to give up his offensive against the Kiso clan, leaving a guard force under the command of Kurihara Akifuyu and Tada Mitsuyori at the fortress to watch over the road to Fukushima in Kiso before marching north on April 6.

## THE SECOND BATTLE AT KAWANAKAJIMA - 1555

In April 1555 Uesugi Kenshin made his way to Zenkôji on the Kawanakajima Plain. Kenshin's goal was Asahiyama Castle, which the Kurita family held. Kenshin made camp near the Zenkôji temple, little more than 1 kilometer northeast of Asahiyama (Mount Asahi). Zenkôji was originally a temple, but the area now functioned as Kenshin's southern border in Shinano, reinforced so that it more closely resembled a fortress than the temple it had once been. Zenkôji formed an important point in the line of defense, but Kenshin utilized Yokoyama Castle, which was nearly on top of the Zenkôji temple, as his main headquarters. A row of fortifications and another castle under Kenshin's control lay in a line running north from Zenkôji.

One of the most skilful diplomats Shingen had assigned to persuading the families in northern Shinano to change sides was Amari Masatada, who had managed to persuade Kurita to switch sides. This had been a relatively easy task, perhaps because Kurita was displeased with what Kenshin had to offer. Kenshin quickly replied to this treacherous act by sending troops against his once loyal vassal not only to quell his rebellious actions, but as an example for the other allies who contemplated going over to the Takeda side. Kenshin's main problem was the desertions of his allies and vassals to the Takeda banner. First Kitajô and now Kurita (Originally, there was only one Kurita family, but at some point the family split into two entities with one now going over to Takeda), not to mention the smaller families who simply surrendered and switched sides without a fight, were lost to him. Kenshin had been successful in crushing Kitajô's attempt at rebellion (maybe he should have set an example at Kitajô), but on this occasion Shingen was making his way to help Kurita, and this would present a completely different situation.

As soon as Kurita heard the Uesugi army was on the march, he sent a messenger to Takeda requesting assistance. Shingen answered by setting off from Tsutsujigasaki on April 24. The sources disagree here: some state Shingen was already in Shinano at this time, because just before Uesugi turned up at Kawanakajima, Shingen had started a campaign against the Kiso clan in western Shinano. This could be true as it seems some of the Takeda army's campaigns were not led directly by Shingen. Newer sources typically assume generals were always in charge of their forces, but it is possible that Shingen handed over command to his senior generals on several occasions, while he himself turned to other urgent issues at hand.

Shingen reached Kawanakajima in July and made camp at Ôtsuka, roughly six kilometers from Kenshin's camp. Patrols from the two camps scouted the area in the hope of spotting the other's position, and if possible thus acquiring an advantage in the terrain for the battle to come. According to the sources,

large forces from the two armies stood on the opposite banks of the River Sai. A point of interest on this occasion is that Imagawa Yoshimoto helped Shingen by sending as many as 3,000 men under the command of Ichinomiya Dewa *no Kami* Munekore to assist Shingen in his campaign against Kenshin in Shinano. This is clear evidence of a solid alliance between the two families. Shingen sent troops to strengthen the defenses at Asahiyama Castle. The reinforcements of 3,000 men sent to Asahiyama included 800 archers and 300 *teppô ashigaru*.

There are a number of critical voices concerning the source *Myôhôji-ki* and the number of 300 *teppô*, because it was only twelve years before that Portuguese merchants had first introduced their *teppô* in Japan. Despite this, the knowledge to build this type of weapon had spread quickly in some areas. Therefore, after a short period of time, weapons were produced in some parts of Japan that were just as good as the imported articles; and since *teppô* were now produced in Japan this increased their availability. Shingen was a rich lord, and could have bought *teppô* early on from producers further west in Japan. The use of *teppô* amongst Takeda's troops as early as 1550 is also mentioned.

There were also reputed to have been hostilities between Uesugi and Takeda on July 19. It was Kenshin who initiated the skirmish by crossing the River Sai. The Uesugi troops were soon in contact with Takeda units in the area near the river. There were clashes, but it did not develop into any decisive battle. Instead things carried on with small engagements, which ended up as a conflict for position.

Fighting morale had sunk to a low level when hostilities were finally ended in October. Both Kenshin and Shingen had hoped that the other would withdraw. It is said that Shingen was in no hurry at the outset, but rather that it was Kenshin who was most interested in a quick victory. However, most of the sources suggest something else, because Shingen sent a letter to the high priest Moriya Yorimasa in Suwa, requiring that Kenshin should withdraw; Moriya was promised an *ando* letter of land areas in the Minochi district. Unfortunaely, Shingen's plea was not heard. A solution to this deadlock between the armies came instead in the form of a peace agreement negotiated by none other than Imagawa Yoshimoto on October 15 between Kenshin and Shingen. The main agreement stipulated that all the families in the area should return to their previous territories, consequently leaving Asahiyama in peace.

Proof of the battle fought on July 19 comes in a so-called *onshô* letter (letter of reward) dated October 5. Kojima Shûri *no Suke* and seven others received letters from Shingen rewarding them for their efforts in the battle on July 19, worth 1,500 *kanmon* in Takanashi in the Takai district of Shinano.

# Chapter 11 - Kiso is Conquered

## KISO YOSHIYASU CAPITULATES

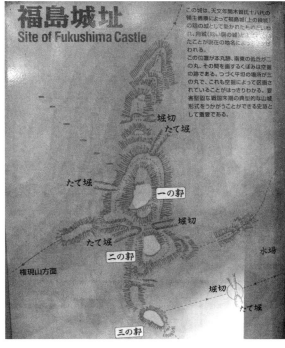

**W**hile the two sides jostled back and forth at Kawanakajima other Takeda generals were also out on campaigns. Once again the Kiso family's castle, Fukushima, in western Chikuma was the target. The winter campaign in February/March had been a fiasco, but now a powerful Takeda army marched yet again through the Torii Pass. Shingen led the army that invaded Kiso, while part of the army remained behind to watch for Uesugi. Shingen, leading the larger part of the Takeda army, crossed the Torii Pass on August 21. The next day Amari Masatada, who commanded the vanguard troops, launched an attack on Fukushima. After some hours fighting Kiso Yoshiyasu and his son, Yoshimasa, surrendered. One source states that Fukushima Castle was besieged for roughly twenty days, the siege ending when Yoshiyasu realized no help was forthcoming.

As part of his surrender, Yoshiyasu agreed to send his daughter to Kôfu as a hostage. In order to strengthen the lord and vassal relationship, Shingen's third daughter was married to Yoshimasa. The Kiso family's land claims were recognized and Kiso was taken up as a member

of the little more than 100 defenders. Once the castle had been captured work was started on its reconstruction. Amakazari became another base for the Takeda clan.

While Sanada was on his campaign on the Kawanakajima Plain, events were unfolding further north. Kenshin had declared that he planned to withdraw from public life, a piece of startling news that naturally caused chaos and confusion amongst his vassals. One of these vassals was Ôkuma Tomohide (?-1582) of the Ôkuma family who held Mikaburi Castle in Echigo. He secretly made contact with Takeda Shingen in Kai to change his allegiance. However, it turned out that Kenshin didn't withdraw from public life in the end, but Tomohide stuck to his original decision and raised the flag of rebellion.

He fled to the neighboring province of Etchû, where he mobilized an army. Near the border between Echigo and Etchû, at a place called Komakaeshi, Tomohide's troops clashed with Kenshin's troops, commanded by the generals Ueno Ienari, and Shôda Sadakata. Tomohide was defeated in the battle that followed. He had no possibility of returning home to Echigo, as this would most likely have cost him his head, so he chose to flee to Tsutsujigasaki in Kai. Shingen gave him a warm welcome and kept his promise of support. It didn't take long before Tomohide gained Shingen's full confidence and was rewarded with a high position in the military hierarchy.

According to the source *Kôyô gunkan* Ôkuma Bizen *no Kami* (probably Tomohide) received a position as an *ashigaru* general with the personal command of 30 cavalry and 75 *ashigaru*. He was now a *fudai* member and served in the *hatamoto* unit.

Critical voices have been raised to dispute the information that Tomohide is the same person as Bizen *no Kami*. There are several who believe that Nagahide is actually Bizen *no Kami*. It is certainly possible that Nagahide and Tomohide came from the same district in Echigo, maybe they were members of the same family; but Nagahide is said to have first fled from Echigo to Kai in 1563. The uncertainty, it seems, is caused by the fact that in the source *Kôyô gunkan* there is no reference to the given name in relation to Ôkuma Bizen *no Kami*.

## THE BATTLE FOR SHINANO

The events of 1556 obviously broke the October 1555 peace agreement between Takeda and Uesugi. It seems that from the beginning Shingen never intended to stick to the agreement, but only kept to it as long as it was to his advantage. Apparently, a "shadow war" of diplomacy had been fought in the background from the moment the agreement was signed until it was officially broken through open hostilities.

In January 1557, Uesugi Kenshin sent a letter to the Hachiman temple in the Sarashina district in Shinano, in which he begged the gods for help to drive Shingen out of Shinano. Kenshin was no doubt convinced that Shingen would never be satisfied until the whole of Shinano was under his dominion.

As expected, only a short amount of time passed before Shingen was ready for new military operations to the north in Shinano. The goal - defeating families allied to the Uesugi clan. Takeda decided that Katsurayama Castle in the Minochi district was of great strategic significance and should be attacked. The castle was the base of the so-called Katsurayama unit (Katsurayama-*shû*), which was a part of the Uesugi clan's military organization. The castle location was strategically vital because it controlled the whole of the Zenkôji Plain; in addition it controlled one of the main roads to and from the Echigo province, to the Uesugi clan's territories.

Shingen assigned the task to his general, Baba Nobuharu, and in February an army of roughly 1,000 men marched towards Katsurayama Castle. Once again, the castle was a *yamashiro*, which meant it would not be easy to capture. Conditions were less than optimal, with some winter snow remaining on the ground, but this suited Shingen because it would slow any reinforcements Uesugi sent to the castle's assistance. The castle's commander, an Uesugi general, Ochiai Bitchû *no Kami*, was therefore forced to manage his defenses as best he could, but Ochiai was not alone, he was assisted by another Uesugi general, Odagiri Yukinaga.

The Takeda divisions surrounded Katsurayama on February 13, and laid siege to the castle. Initially things appeared to favor Bitchû *no Kami*, he had the whole of the Ochiai clan on his side full of fighting spirit. Unfortunately, events quickly turned against the commander. Information on what followed is sparse, but it seems that two of his family members, Ochiai Tôtômi *no Kami* and Saburôzaemonnojô, turned traitor before the first blow in the battle was struck, reducing the number of defenders. This was not the only problem the besieged general

Photo TAK 4-41

The Jôshôji Temple located at the foot of Katsurayama Castle.

Photo TAK 4-42 & 4-43

The *honmaru* of Katsurayama Castle.

had to face. The Takeda army also managed to cut off the water supply to the castle. The castle's water came from the Jôshôji temple, located at the foot of Katsurayama. It is said that it was the temple's head priest who had tipped off Takeda about the water supply. Without a replenishing water supply the castle's defenders could only hold out for as long as their stores of water remained. However, the Takeda army didn't plan a long and drawn out siege, but wished to take the castle swiftly by force. To ensure this would happen they had to capture the castle before reinforcements from Uesugi arrived.

On February 15 the Takeda army stormed the castle's defenses, but unfortunately for the Takeda the attack soon came to a standstill. Not only did the scattered snow hinder advance, but dead trees and dry grass covering the mountainside further slowed the Takeda troops. Met by this natural resistance, Shingen tried a new strategy. The grass was set alight and the flames slowly but surely spread upwards towards the castle's fortifications, built mainly from wood and bamboo. The palisades soon started to burn and not long afterwards the Takeda army launched a violent attack on the part of the castle that had been damaged by the fire. One

by one Ochiai's men were put out of action. Bitchû *no Kami* and most of his soldiers were killed in the battle, in total – about 200 men. Some of the civilians, women and children inside Katsurayama, are said to have actively participated in the defense of the castle. To avoid being taken prisoner and sold as slaves, or worse, some of the women jumped to their deaths from the mountain shelves; those that chose not to would meet an even worse fate. Takeda Shingen was very glad when he heard the news of the successful attack, sending out so-called *kanjô* letters to those of his soldiers who had fought bravely on March 10.

News of this brutal assault reached Uesugi Kenshin quickly. He leapt into action and initiated a crisis plan. A letter of mobilization was sent out on February 16 to Irobe Katsunaga, one of his generals. Information is limited on whether or not Katsunaga actually went to help the Ochiai family's defenses. He may not have gone to the castle's assistance after receiving news that the castle had already fallen.

With the victory over Katsurayama most of the Zenkôji plain, which was northeast of Kawanakajima, was now in Takeda's hands. Kenshin's countermeasures involved mobilizing his vassals and allies by letter; he was unable to participate himself at the time. The seriousness of this latest Takeda incursion became clear to Kenshin when Takanashi Masayori, lord of Iiyama, informed him that Iiyama Castle in the very northeast of Shinano in the Takai district was the target for an advancing Takeda army. In the letter Masayori asked Kenshin for help; Kenshin answered by ordering Nagao Masakage to march out on March 23, while Kenshin planned to set off from Kasugayama the next day. At least this was his original plan. Kenshin seems to have dawdled in these matters because the sources indicate he crossed the border into Shinano no earlier than April 18. This could have been part of his strategy and not just slow mobilization on his part. He then advanced further towards the Zenkôji Plain, setting up camp in the area on April 21. He dispatched soldiers to recapture fortresses in the Takai district, with Yamada and Fukushima being two of several fortresses subsequently captured. While his troops moved south, Kenshin also moved camp. Kenshin used Asahiyama Castle (taken April 25) as his main headquarters, and for a period his soldiers were occupied with the restoration of the castle.

Takeda Shingen is said to have stayed at Kôfu while all of this activity was taking place. On March 11 a letter was sent from Kijima Izumo *no Kami* informing Shingen that parts of the Uesugi army were now on the move. Shingen received the letter three days later, on March 14, at Tsutsujigasaki but remained relatively calm. However, he sent mobilization orders to his generals in the north. During this period Shingen was often involved in various conflicts and battles in different parts of the country and it was impossible for him to be personally involved in all of them. Therefore he time and again conveyed orders to generals and families in the areas concerned to deal with any aggression. His generals were capable, and he trusted them to follow out whatever orders he sent to them.

After having consolidated his position on Kawanakajima, Uesugi's army made ready to advance further south. The campaign started on May 12, with most of the action occurring in the Hanishina district. All the castles and fortresses under Takeda control in the area were attacked and captured. It was not long, therefore, before large parts of the area were under Kenshin's control. However, Kenshin chose to break off his campaign to the southwest and instead turned his sights on Iiyama.

Kenshin's target was the Ichikawa family in the Takai district who had gone over to Takeda. One explanation why Kenshin suddenly turned around might have been that he wanted to be sure a guard was in place to protect his flanks before advancing further to the south. For Ichikawa's part there seemed to be little hope in trying to stand against Kenshin's powerful army on his own, so he sent a messenger asking Shingen for help. Shingen answered this call by ordering Sanada Yukitaka to take his own force, as well as the 500 *ashigaru* stationed at Shioda Castle in Ueda, to Ichikawa's aid. What happened next is unclear, because information on further developments is a bit vague. It seems that Kenshin chose to withdraw from Iiyama Castle, his mission abandoned. This respite was a short one, however, because Kenshin soon dispatched troops to the south again, attacking enemy divisions in the areas near Sakaki and Iwahana, west of Ueda (this was possibly Sanada Yukitaka's troops) on May 15. The Takeda forces were defeated, but did not suffer especially large losses.

Wherever possible, Shingen used diplomacy to solve conflicts, but it was a policy which now and then had to be backed up with military power. For instance, on July 5, the Takeda attacked the strategically important Otari Castle, which lay to the very north of the Azumi district, on the border between Shinano and Echigo. The attack was successful and yet another enemy fortress was now in the hands of Takeda. With this victory the Takeda army could now threaten the enemy by attacking them from the rear. Such strategic zigzagging and fighting for key positions happened frequently. In addition, Shingen endeavored to weaken the alliance between Kenshin and his vassals and his allies, preferably without using military might. All this diplomatic maneuvering points to Shingen not being interested in any decisive battle with Kenshin at this point in time.

**Illustration 4-17**.

A *nanbandô gusoku* (a southern barbarian armor). As the translation of the name suggests, this suit of armor was inspired by the European style – a cuirass. It appeared during the Sengoku Period when the first European ships came to Japan (1542/43). This was also the year Japanese samurai saw the European *teppô* for the first time. The *dô* was designed to resist *teppô* bullets, and was tested to do just that before the wearer used the armor in battle. Therefore many of the suits still in existence today show where bullets left their mark.

# Chapter 13 - Moving East

## TAKEDA INVADES KÔZUKE

**S**hingen had been engaged in military campaigns in the north since 1542, but was yet to conquer the whole of Shinano. However, he had managed to take large parts of the province, and thereby also controlled the gateways to other provinces. Kôzuke, which lay to the west of the Saku district, was one such border province. Shingen now controlled some of the roads leading into Kôzuke and with them an invasion route. After the relatively unsuccessful campaign against Uesugi it is possible Shingen wanted to try his luck in other areas. Another reason may have been that Shingen had received information that Kenshin was also interested in this area in the east, and perhaps Shingen wanted to hinder Kenshin gaining influence in Kôzuke.

**Photo TAK 4-44**

The *honmaru* of Minowa Castle. Minowa was a huge castle and controlled the central parts of Kôzuke. It was held by the Nagano family until the Takeda captured it in 1566. At the time of the author's visit, major excavations were under way.

**Photo TAK 4-45**

A part of the dry moats around, and in between, the various compounds of Minowa Castle. They were huge and between 8 to 10 meters deep. With a wooden or bamboo fence along the upper ridge the fortress would be difficult to attack.

The Takeda army marched towards Kôzuke in April 1557. Unfortunately, detailed information in the sources is sparse, but the main aim of the imminent campaign was Minowa Castle, held by Nagano Narimasa. The Nagano clan had been vassals of the Uesugi clan on the Kantô Plain for a long time, but the family were given a free hand in their rule over significant areas of land. This meant they could mobilize a considerable force, but was still small when compared to the Takeda army. The mission of attacking Minowa fell to

Takeda Yoshinobu, Shingen's son. Yoshinobu is said to have led an army of 13,000 men. However, despite the size of the Takeda force, the campaign ended in a fiasco. The defenders were extremely effective in repulsing the castle's attackers, time and time again pushing the Takeda force back. Tail between his legs, the young commander withdrew his men and returned to Kai. How his father reacted to his young warrior son's embarrassing defeat is not known, but his reaction must have been anything but pleasant.

## THE THIRD BATTLE AT KAWANAKAJIMA - 1557

The action on the Kawanakajima Plain finally reached a climax in the late summer. Shingen is said to have led an army of roughly 23,000 men across the plain, while Kenshin had only about 10,000 men under his command. Apparently, Shingen had avoided a decisive battle with Kenshin for several months; something difficult to make sense of considering the difference in the sizes of their forces. A decisive battle was about to be fought, but once again, its outcome would be anything but final for these two old enemies.

According to so-called *kanjô* letters from the Uesugi clan, a battle is said to have taken place at the beginning of August (another source records this as the end of August) on the Uenohara Plain, which lies in the northern part of Kawanakajima, in the Minochi district roughly 4 kilometers northeast of the Zenkôji plain. It is difficult to pinpoint the exact location of the battle because different accounts exist. One of these accounts states that the battle was fought on the Higanohara plain. It is also speculated that the battle was fought in the areas of Iizuna and Togakushi. The battle is also said to have been fought at night, something which might explain why the clash was limited, but again sparse information makes this difficult to confirm.

The reason for this battle is said to be that Shingen tried to avoid Kenshin's positions in order to advance along the Chikuni road and up towards the border between Shinano and Echigo with the intention of cutting off Kenshin's lines of supply. Another version says it was to attack Kasugayama Castle itself; it is possible a combination of both these plans was in effect as well. Kenshin at least received news of the situation and dispatched troops to prevent the Takeda troops from reaching their goal. Once again this developed into a positional battle between the two sides, where the only action of note was the movement of troops, something neither side was very happy about.

However, at the beginning of September, Kenshin suddenly withdrew his men to Echigo. Shingen stayed a little longer in the area, but at the beginning of October he ordered his army back to Kôfu. It is said that the *Shôgun* Ashikaga Yoshiteru

Photo TAK 4-46

A Zunari-*kabuto* and a *teppô* awaiting their samurai owner. (Shingen-kô festival in Kôfu).

Photo TAK 4-47

Five samurai with *teppô* ready to move out. During the 1550s the use of *teppô* began to spread, creating a high demand for *teppô* already manufactured. It seems that the Takeda clan was forced to purchase this weapon, since there is no clear evidence of any *teppô* production within their territories. (Shingen-kô festival in Kôfu).

was the reason for this change in the situation; he is said to have functioned as a kind of mediator between the two sides. However this is not the most likely explanation, because evidence exists that Yoshiteru in fact asked Kenshin to come to Kyôto, thus explaining why he suddenly withdrew his forces. This action is a likely explanation of how Yoshiteru solved the problem of the positional war on Kawanakajima.

# Chapter 14 – A New Ruler

## SHINGEN'S SHINANO

After the third battle at Kawanakajima the situation seems just as confused as it was before the campaign. However, in the history books Shingen is credited with victory, which seems to be the correct conclusion to reach, because in the spring of 1558 (or 1559) Shingen was appointed *Shugo* of Shinano. The Ogasawara family had been deposed, and the position was vacant. It seemed completely natural, for Shingen at least, that he be appointed to this position, given that he now controlled nearly the whole of Shinano. It is likely that the Takeda clan lobbied the *Shôgun* Yoshiteru in Kyôto a great deal concerning this matter. In a letter to Yoshiteru, dated November 28, Shingen gave an account of the invasions of Shinano, an account that naturally contained little self-criticism.

**Illustration 4-18.**

*Tatami-gusoku* (folding armor). As the name suggests, the *tatami-gusoku* was a snap to store away. A soldier simply folded it up and placed in a small box or made it in to a small bundle. Exactly when it first appeared is difficult to say, but it was in wide use during the Sengoku Period among lower class warriors and *ashigaru*, as well as with cavalry samurai who used it as a summer uniform. Suits were either metal or leather plates sewn onto a piece of cloth. To strengthen the armor chain-mail was used to connect the plates together, helping to retain the armor's flexibility.

In the meantime, Shingen had tightened his grip on Shinano by the establishing of so-called *zaiban-shû* (stationary units): Kashiwabachi Castle in the Minochi district, Ôka Castle in the Sarashina district, and Amakazari and Higashijô Castles in the Hanishina district. Although not all the fortresses and castles in Shinano had been captured, his control of the key points suggests that Shingen finally had dominion over the Shinano province. While tightening his grip on northern Shinano by appointing castle lords, Shingen also issued orders that were unusual: he ordered that the Zenkôji temple in Sarashina be moved to the Yamanashi district in Kai; as far as the author can see this did not concern the whole temple complex, but only some parts of it, such as the *honzon* (principal image). Now and then Shingen received orders from unexpected quarters. For instance, Emperor Ôgimachi requested (January 11, 1558) that Shingen repair the Buneiji temple at Chiku in the Ina district in Shinano. The Buneiji temple had been burned to the ground during the Takeda invasion of the Ina district in 1554. Shingen responded to the request by giving land areas to the temple so that a new building could be constructed.

Autumn of 1558 was a peaceful period for Shingen, and he spent much of his time together with his family in Tsutsujigasaki.

Here ends the second book on Takeda Shingen, but the story of Shingen continues in book five in the *Saga of the Samurai* series including the exciting fourth battle at Kawanakajima (1561). Book five will also look more closely at the Takeda *shinobi* division, and at whether the so-called *kagemusha* story is rooted in credible sources. In addition, the Takeda clan's law books called *Kôshû hatto no shidai* will be reviewed.

**Illustration 4-19.**

A *teppô* samurai. The samurai prepares his gun by pouring powder into the pan. This *teppô* was one of the heavier styles in use during the Sengoku Period. Weather and rain were a *teppô* soldier's worst enemies. When fighting in the open the *teppô* soldier depended on a stockade or some other protection, because by the time he reloaded and was ready to fire again the enemy might run him down. The soldier wears a typical *okegawa-dô*.

**Illustration 4-20.**

A *hôrokubiya* (a grenade/bomb). An *ashigaru* throws an *hôrokubiya* towards enemy positions. The origin of this type of weapon goes far back to China. In Japan it came into use during the later half of the Sengoku Period, but little information exists on these grenades making it difficult to say if they were ever used in mass. Styles varied, with the casing typically made of leather, paper, ceramic, or metal. This *ashigaru* wears a *jinbaori* over his armor and a *katana* sword in his belt – he is a typical early Edo Period warrior.

| | |
|---|---|
| *Abumi* | stirrups. |
| *Ando* | letter given to a person/family as confirmation that land areas are still in their possession, literally translated as *relief*. |
| *Ashiyowa* | literally meaning "unsteady legs." May be interpreted as old people, women and children. |
| *Bajô-yari* | cavalry spear. |
| *Bugyô* | a magistrate. |
| *Chokkatsu-chi* | an area of land under direct control of the *daimyô*. |
| *Fudai* | hereditary vassal (an insider, as opposed to *tozama* - an outsider). |
| *Gundai* | district deputy. |
| *Honzon* | the principal image of a temple. |
| *Ikki* | a group of farmers and low-class samurai who joined together in armed units. Together they often instigated rebellions. |
| *Ji-samurai* | "samurai of the soil." Relatively poor independent samurai who ruled over a small area of land, or had a small income from their lord; the lowest ranking warriors, but above the *ashigaru*. |
| *Jitô* | a steward - the lord of a manor. |
| *Jôdai* | a deputy governor/commander of a castle. |
| *Kanjô* | a letter of thanks; a lord's letter to a retainer that have served him well during a campaign; a letter of recognition of exploits. |
| *Karyôsen* | a correctional fine. |
| *Konida-tai* | a baggage train/supply train. |
| *Kuni-shû* | country units, military units from the districts. |
| *Kuwadate* | a ground-breaking ceremony, same as *kuwaire*. |
| *Kuwaire* | a ground-breaking ceremony, same as *kuwadate*. |
| *Maki* | a meadow/pasture, in Japan often associated with the area for breeding horses. |
| *Nagamaki* | a short spear shaft with a long sword blade attached, sometimes referred to as a straight *naginata*. |
| *Naginata* | a glaive, a spear shaft with a curved blade attached. |
| *Nigura* | a packsaddle. |
| *Onsen* | a hot spring, a spa. |
| *Onshô* | a reward. |
| *Rônin* | a masterless samurai, a warrior with no income. |
| *Shijô* | support castle, also known as *tsumejiro* or *edajiro*. |
| *Shinobi* | spies, sometimes also called *ninja* or *kanja* (but a *ninja* was more usually an assassin). |
| *Shinrui-shû* | a family member, also known as *shinzoku-shû*. |
| *Tachi* | a sword worn with the cutting-edge downwards. |
| *Tantô* | a dagger. |
| *Tozama* | an outsider, the opposite of a *fudai* vassal. |
| *Utokusen* | a form of tax, also known as *tokuyakusen* and *utokuyaku*. |
| *Wa-abumi* | circle or ring stirrups, used before the Nara period. |
| *Waraji* | straw sandals. |
| *Yamashiro* | a mountain castle. |
| *Zaijô-shû* | a stationed castle unit, soldiers serving at a specific castle. |

This personality index presents the Takeda clan's opponents from 1510 to roughly 1560.

## FUJISAWA YORICHIKA (?)

Lord of Fukuyo Castle, situated in the Ina district in the Shinano province. His mother and father are not known. We know little of Yorichika or his family, but the source *Kai kokushi* states that Fujisawa in Shinano is a branch of the Fujisawa clan in the Sagami province. Fujisawa is said to have served the *Shugo* family, Ogasawara, in Shinano before ending up as lord of Fukuyo Castle; but in the 1540s events developed rapidly. Takeda Shingen had targeted the Shinano province, and he was soon marching north with his army towards the Suwa and Ina districts. The first Takeda attack on Fukuyo was carried out in 1544; Takeda's defeat enabled Yorichika to rule for yet another year. When a much larger Takeda force attacked Fukuyo Yorichika was forced to make peace and open the gates, becoming a Takeda vassal. The next time he appears in the sources is in September 1545, when Takeda Shingen is at war against the Hôjô clan from Odawara. Where and when Yorichika died is not known.

## HÔJÔ UJITSUNA (1486-1541)

Lord of Odawara Castle, located in the Ashigara-shimo district in the Sagami province. He was the son of Hôjô (Ise) Sôun, his mother is unknown. Other names and titles Ujitsuna used were Chiyomaru, Shinkurô, Ise Ujitsuna, and Sakyônodayû. He took over the Hôjô clan in August 1518, only one year before his father died. Ujitsuna moved from Nirayama Castle, which had been Hôjô Sôun's headquarters for many years. Odawara became the new base; it lay further to the east, on the other side of the Hakone Pass. In 1524 he changed the family name to Hôjô, and from then on the clan at Odawara Castle was called Hôjô. Like his father, Ujitsuna had territorial ambitions, quickly launching into military campaigns against his neighbors. The campaigns bore fruit and gradually the Hôjô territories grew larger. On several occasions (1524, 1525, 1526 and 1535) there were military confrontations with the Takeda clan. For most of his life Ujitsuna was involved in military campaigns. He died on July 17, 1541, after a period of sickness. His grave can be found at Sôunji ("ji" meaning "temple," or in other words, at Sôun temple) in the town of Hakone.

## HÔJÔ UJIYASU (1515-1571)

Lord of Odawara Castle, located in the Ashigara-shimo district in the Sagami province. He was the son of Hôjô Ujitsuna, his mother is unknown. Other names and titles he used were: Izu Chiyomaru, Shinkurô, Sagami *no Kami*, Taseiken (?), and Sakyônodayû. When his father died in 1541 he took over as head of the Hôjô family, becoming the second generation of Hôjô lords at Odawara Castle. Ujiyasu soon had ambitions for his new domain; amongst these was a new system of taxes. He also launched military projects, such as the development of a comprehensive network of support forts, whose purpose was to protect the Hôjô clan's territories. In 1554 a peace agreement in which all parties would concentrate their efforts on other fronts for an indefinite number of years was reached between the Imagawa, Takeda, and Hôjô families. Ujiyasu exploited this opportunity well, launching military campaigns to the east and northeast. In 1568 Shingen attacked the Imagawa family in Suruga and the alliance between the three clans was broken. The year after Shingen invaded the Sagami province, going to war with the Hôjô family. For the last year of his life Ujiyasu was at war with Takeda without any decisive result being reached. He died on October 3, 1571. It is said that he was paralyzed for some time before his death. His grave can be found at the Sôunji temple in the town of Hakone.

## IMAGAWA UJICHIKA (1471 OR 1473-1526)

Lord of Sunpu Castle, located in the Uto district in the Suruga province. He was the first-born son of Imagawa Yoshitada. His mother was Kitagawa-dono, older sister of Hôjô Sôun. Other names he used include Tatsuômaru (Ryûômaru), Hikogorô, Shûridayû, Jibudayû(?), Kazusa *no Suke*, Shôki, and Kyôsan. Ujichika was only five years old when his father died in 1476, creating an inheritance conflict within the family. A certain Oshika Norimitsu who appeared on the scene functioned as a kind of warden or substitute leader. As has often happened throughout history, persons who rule on behalf of their wards are reluctant to give up their power once the child comes of age. The family soon divided into two groups, one group supporting Ujichika and the other Norimitsu. The divide worsened over the years, but in 1487, with support of Hôjô Sôun, Ujichika attacked Norimitsu in his Sunpu manor, and Norimitsu was killed. Ujichika now became the ruling lord of the Imagawa family, and for much of the rest of his life he was at war with the Takeda clan in Kai. He died on June 23, 1526. Ujichika's grave can be found at the Zôzenji temple in the town of Shizuoka.

## IMAGAWA UJITERU (1513-1536)

Lord of Sunpu Castle, located in the Uto district in the Suruga province. He was the first-born son of Ujichika. His mother was Jukeini (?-1568), the daughter of Nakamikado Nobutane (1442-1525) - a *Kugyô* member. Other names and titles he used were Tatsuômaru, Gorô, Jûgoinoge, and Kazusa *no Suke*. When Ujichika died in 1526, Ujiteru was first in line to inherit the position as head of the Imagawa clan. During his period as clan leader he led a number of military campaigns against Takeda in the north, but without any great success. After only ten years as head of the family Ujiteru died at Sunpu Castle. The cause of death is uncertain, but it is speculated that he died from some kind of sickness, on March 17. He is buried at Rinzaiji temple in Shizuoka town.

## IMAGAWA YOSHIMOTO (1519-1560)

Lord of Sunpu Castle, located in the Uto district in the Suruga province. He was the fifth (another source states the third) son of Ujichika. His mother was Jukeini (?-1568). Other names and titles which Yoshimoto used were Hôgikumaru, Kazusa *no Suke*, Jibudayû(?), Ju-shi-i-no-ge, Baigaku Shôhô, and Mikawa *no Kami*. His brother, Ujiteru, was the first-born son of Ujichika, taking over as head of the family when their father died in 1526. Ten years later, however, Ujiteru died leaving the position vacant. The next in line, Hikogorô, had also died the same day. Two other sons had been sent to a temple, Genkô Etan (Yoshimasa) and Senjô (or Sensô), so it appeared that it would be the fifth born, Yoshimoto, who would inherit the position as leader of the clan.

A dispute concerning the succession, which became known as Hanakura-*no-ran* (the Hanakura Rebellion), arose and parties sided either with Yoshimoto or his elder brother, Genkô Etan. Because Etan's mother came from the Kushima family, a vassal family of Imagawa, she was most likely a concubine. Because of this, Etan was most likely considered an illegitimate child and not in the direct line of succession. This is one explanation for why Yoshimoto considered it his right to become head of the family when two of his elder and legitimate brothers had passed away, with a third sent to a temple. The fourth, Etan, had also been sent to a temple, but had not given up worldly affairs. In medieval Japan it was not unusual for a person to be religious and belong to a temple, yet at the same time engage in acts of brutality, such as cutting down one's enemies with a sword.

It was in this conflict that Takeda Nobutora supported Yoshimoto, something that provided a foundation for the future cooperation between the two clans. It is difficult to say how important Takeda's support was for Yoshimoto's victory, but evidence suggests that without Shingen's military support Yoshimoto probably wouldn't have been victorious. Yoshimoto, then, became the new Imagawa lord in the late summer of 1536. He secured his areas and gradually conquered more and more land to the detriment of his neighbors, but not against his good neighbor in the north, the Takeda clan. For the next ten years Yoshimoto expanded steadily to the west. The climax came in the year 1560, when Yoshimoto invaded the Owari Province with 25,000 men. There he clashed with Oda Nobunaga, who only commanded roughly 2,500 soldiers; nevertheless, Yoshimoto suffered a colossal defeat at the battle near Okehazama on May 19, 1560, in which he lost his head and with it the rang death knell of the Imagawa clan.

## KASAHARA KIYOSHIGE (?-1547)

Lord of Shiga Castle, situated in the Saku district in the Shinano province. It is not known who his mother and father were. The other names he used were Shinsaburô, and Masatomo. As far as the origin of the Kasahara clan is concerned, there were many families called Kasahara, but the name of the family in Saku may originate from two villages in the Shinano province, in the districts Takai and Ina. It is perhaps possible to trace the roots of Kasahara Kiyoshige back to Kasahara Yorinao, who took part in the Taira clan's military engagement in the Genpei War (1180-1185); but whether Kasahara is a branch of Taira is difficult to say. The family is said to have served under *Shikken*, Hôjô Yoshitoki (1163-1224), in Kamakura, but at one time during the Kenpô Period (1213-1218) the family is said to have moved to Saku in Shinano. A possible connection to Suwa through the Suwa clan's Jin family in Shinano is mentioned as a possible origin of the family. The Kasahara family in Saku are also said to have been called Yoda.

When Takeda Shingen invaded the Saku district in Shinano in 1547, the Kasahara family at Shiga Castle decided to resist. The result was inevitable: Kiyoshige was either killed or he committed *seppuku* together with his two young children. Women and children were typically taken prisoner and sold as slaves under the direction of Oyamada Nobuari, but this episode is said to have blackened the future reputation of Shingen.

## MURAKAMI YOSHIKIYO (1501 OR 1503-1573)

Lord of Katsurao Castle, located in the Hanishina district in the Shinano province. His father was Yorihira, who was the nineteenth generation of Murakami clan leaders. His mother is unknown. Other names and titles Yoshikiyo used were Takeômaru, Saemonnojô, and Suô *no Kami*. Up until the Takeda family's invasion in 1542, the Murakami clan had functioned as one of the 'two large clans' in Shinano, the other being the Ogasawara clan. Murakami Yoshikiyo was the twenty-first generation of the Murakami clan, who had been active in Shinano for centuries. The clan's influence had gradually increased in the Shinano districts, and in the sixteenth century the clan had interests in six districts, with Murakami maintaining full control over some of these. Yoshikiyo had inherited the clan's warlike attitude, and was a skilful general and strategist. It was also he who had inflicted the first defeat on Shingen in 1548. However, unfortunately for Yoshikiyo, Shingen did not give up so easily, and in the end the Murakami clan was chased out of Shinano. The rest of his life Yoshikiyo was close to the Uesugi clan, taking part in military campaigns against Takeda's forces in Shinano time and time again. Uesugi took part in the famous battle on the Kawanakajima Plain in 1561, but was not victorious and never managed to recapture his earlier territories. Yoshikiyo died on January 1, 1573 at Nechi Castle in the Kubiki district in Echigo (although another source states Akazawa Castle in the Uonuma district).

## ÔI NOBUSATO (1468?-?)

Lord of Ueno Castle in the Koma district in the Kai province. His father was Ôi Nobukane. His mother is unknown. He also went by the name Sôgei. Like the Takeda family, the Ôi family could trace their roots back to Shinrasaburô Yoshimitsu. Because of this common origin they coexisted and ruled their own areas without any serious confrontations. Only when Nobutora came to power in the sixteenth century did they engage in armed conflict with one another. At that time Nobusato was head of the Ôi clan, refusing to bend to pressure from the Takeda clan. But after his defeat at Imasuwa in 1520, he was forced to give up. It is said that he went into the service of Takeda, and that he moved to the Tsutsujigasaki Estate. Here he supposedly spent the rest of his life serving Nobutora, but for how long is a mystery, because the date of his death is unknown.

## OGASAWARA NAGATOKI (1514-1583)

Lord of Hayashi Castle, located in the Chikuma district in the Shinano province. He was the first-born son of Ogasawara Nagamune, who was lord of Fukashi Castle. His mother is unknown. The other names and titles he used were Hômatsumaru(?), Matajirô, Uma *no Suke*, Gokosessai(?), Daizendaibu, Shinano *no Kami*, Jugoinojô(?), and Shinano *no Shugo*. It should be mentioned that up through the seventeenth century the Ogasawara spread throughout several provinces in Japan, but this particular branch came originally from the Kai province. The family name is said to stem from the village of the same name in Kai, but the family later moved to Shinano. In Shinano the Ogasawara clan ruled over the districts Azumi and Chikuma. Everything seemed to be going well for the Ogasawara until Takeda Shingen invaded Shinano in 1542. Before the Takeda invasion, the Ogasawara clan had more or

less been concerned with small military campaigns against local families. But after the Takeda family's appearance they were put under extreme pressure, with every ounce of their strength devoted to stopping the wave of aggression from the south. In 1548 Nagatoki and Shingen met near the Shiojiri Pass and Ogasawara suffered a thundering defeat. The family never recovered completely from this defeat and struggled long for survival after Nagatoki surrendered Hayashi and fled. In the end, Shingen took over the position of *Shugo* of Shinano, thereby making the Ogasawara clan's defeat total. Nagatoki wandered around for a period as a *rônin*, but in 1555 he is said to have made contact with other branches of his Ogasawara family and ended up in Kyôto. In Kyôto he banded together with Miyoshi Nagayoshi (also called Chôkei); but when Miyoshi died in 1564, Nagatoki traveled to Echigo - to the Uesugi clan. Here he was given an income of 500 *kan*, but after Kenshin's death in 1578 he sought the Ashina family who lived in Aizu Wakamatsu in the Mutsu province. Nagatoki lived there until he died, February 25, 1583. His grave can be found at the Keizanji temple.

## SUWA YORIMITSU (1479/80-1539)

Lord of Uehara Castle in the Suwa district in the Shinano province. Yorimitsu was the second son of Masamitsu. His mother is unknown. The other names and titles he used were Hekiunsai, and Miyahôshi-maru. The Suwa clan could trace its roots back to the Ôhafuri (Ôhôri) clan, which functioned as a religious leadership for the Suwa Taisha temple. At the end of the Nanbokuchô Period the clan split with one part becoming more of a pure military family, namely the Suwa. On January 8, 1483 his father and elder brother were invited to Ôhafuri Tsugumitsu's temple manor. They were invited to a *sake* feast, but things didn't turn out quite as Yorimitsu's father had expected, he and his son were instead killed in an ambush. Tsugumitsu was trying to achieve full control of the region, but the Suwa clan's vassals strongly disliked Tsugumitsu's way of doing things. Therefore it didn't take very long before Tsugumitsu felt threatened and insecure. He chose to flee and sought refuge in the areas near Takatô, in the Ina district.

In December 1484 the young Yorimitsu was appointed as head of the Ôhafuri family and Suwa. However, Tsugumitsu had not quite given up his goal of control, and the conflict continued until 1487. Afer hostilities ended Suwa Yorimitsu was now in charge, defeating the Kanasashi family of Shimo Suwa in 1518 and taking complete control of the Suwa district. In 1528 Suwa was threatened by the Takeda clan, but Yorimitsu led his forces brilliantly forcing Takeda into retreat. In 1531 it was Yorimitsu who invaded Kai, unfortunately without success. In 1535 a peace agreement was signed. After having fallen ill with some sort of kind of swelling on his back, Yorimitsu died in December 1539.

## SUWA YORISHIGE (1516-1542)

Lord of Uehara Castle in the Suwa district in Shinano province. The oldest son of Suwa Yoritaka. His mother is unknown. Also known as Gyôbudayû. His father, Yoritaka, died in 1530, therefore he took over the family when his grandfather, Yorimitsu, died in 1539. Because he was married to Shingen's sister, he felt a good foundation had been laid for peace between the two families. However, Yorishige was frightfully mistaken. In the summer of 1542 Shingen invaded the Suwa district, forcing Yorishige to surrender. He was taken prisoner and sent to Kôfu, where he was ordered to commit *seppuku* on July 21 (another source states the evening of July 20). His grave can be found at the Tôkôji temple in Kôfu, Yamanashi prefecture.

## TAKANASHI MASAYORI (?)

Lord of Takanashi Castle in the Takai district in Shinano province. Masayori was the son of Sumiyori. His mother is unknown. The Takanashi family was a branch of the Inoue family and could trace its roots back to the Minamoto clan. The family's castle/estate was originally in Nakano-Otate (later called Takanashi Castle). The family became more prominent at the end of the Nanbokuchô period; and like all other families in Japan during this time were involved in conflicts involving land. The Sengoku Period was a turbulent time, especially between 1555 and 1559. During this time Takanashi was put under extreme pressure by the culprit of so many difficulties for the families in Shinano - the Takeda clan. Masayori chose to use Iiyama Castle as his headquarters. On several occasions Masayori entered into a coalition against Takeda, but it was no use, because in 1559 the Takeda army attacked Takanashi Castle, forcing Masayori to flee. The date and cause of his death are unknown. His descendants went into service with the Uesugi clan.

## UESUGI KENSHIN (1530-1578)

Lord of Kasugayama Castle in the Kubiki district in Echigo province. Kenshin was the third son of *Shugo-dai* Nagao Tamekage in Echigo. His mother's name was Toragozen. Other names and titles Kenshin used were Torachiyo, Nagao Heisô Kagetora, Masatora, Terutora, Fushikian Kenshin, Sôshin, Danjôshôhitsu, and *Kantô kanrei*. Kenshin's father died as early as 1536, and Harukage, the first-born son, became the head of the family. In 1543 Torachiyo underwent his *genpuku* ceremony, taking the name Nagao Kagetora. In 1545 a vassal of the Uesugi clan killed his other brother, Kageyasu. This was a dangerous period for Kagetora, but he came through it unscathed. Unfortunately, things were not well within the family; Kagetora and his eldest brother did not get along, and gradually the struggle to gain allies began.

In 1548 growing tensions between the two brothers spilled over into armed conflict; but *Shugo* Uesugi Sadazane became involved and managed to arrange an agreement. The agreement was not very advantageous to Harukage, but he suffered from some sickness and chose to withdraw from public life rather than continue to fight his brother. Kagetora was appointed head of the family and moved to Kasugayama. Sadazane died two years after this take over, and since he didn't have any children the *Shugo* family died out. The real power in Echigo now went to Nagao Kagetora (Kenshin), but this resulted in a good deal of campaigns with other clans in Echigo who were unwilling to immediately recognize the new leader. Unfortunately, they were unable to stop Kagetora and instead offered the choice of surrender or annihilation. In 1552 *Kantô kanrei* Uesugi Norimasa was chased out of the Kantô Plain by the Hôjô clan in Odawara. When Norimasa sought refuge with Kagetora in Echigo the clan leader asked in return only the deposed *Kantô kanrei* adopt him. Norimasa agreed to this with the official adoption taking place in the summer of 1561 in Kamakura town. Nagao Kagetora then changed his name to Uesugi Masatora. He received the 'Masa' part of the name from his adopted father, Norimasa.

In the 1550s Uesugi became involved in a conflict with Takeda from Kai. For more than a decade the two great clans fought almost constant military campaigns on the Kawanakajima Plain in Shinano. In addition to campaigns against Takeda in Shinano, Kagetora's attention was occupied with campaigns on the Kantô Plain, in provinces such as Etchû, Kôzuke, and Shimotsuke. A little while after he set off towards the Kantô Plain he suffered a stroke on March 9, 1578. He died four days later on March 13. Kenshin had amassed extensive territory during his life, territory he bequeathed to his two adopted sons. He was buried at Fushikiin in the Kasugayama Castle.

As far as the source material concerning the battles at Kawanakajima goes, they present diverging views concerning not only how many confrontations actually took place, but also the dates when they took place. These discrepancies exist regardless of whether the Takeda or the Uesugi sources are referenced.

## SOURCES AND DATES REFERRING TO LARGE AND SMALL BATTLES ON THE KAWANAKAJIMA PLAIN

### UESUGI

*Kawanakajima godo kassen no shidai* - 1553, 1554, 1556, 1557, and 1561.
*Uesugi nenpu* - 1553, 1556, and 1561.
The newly discovered Kawanakajima folding screen - 1554, 1556.

### TAKEDA

*Kôhakusai-ki* – 1552, and 1553.
*Kôyô gunkan* – 1552-1555, 1557-1561, and 1564.
*Myôhôji-ki* – 1552-1555, and 1561.

### OTHER SOURCES

A folding screen at the Nishimura museum – 1561.
The history of Nagano city *Nagano shishi* – 1555, 1557, and 1561.
Other letters and documents from the period – 1552-1559, 1561 and 1564.

Common between the above sources are five dates which, in retrospect, have been recognized as armed confrontations on the Kawanakajima Plain between Takeda and Uesugi: 1553, 1555, 1557, 1561, and 1564. But these five "recognized" dates might have been accepted mainly because of the actual location of the battles. However, some of the confrontations took place on, outside, and/or near the border of what is understood to be the Kawanakajima Plain, but are not considered battles on Kawanakajima in any of the sources - for instance in the year

1552. As far as the sources on the Uesugi side are concerned, none refer to 1564. This year is mentioned in the Takeda sources, and the so-called "other sources." But the confrontation in 1564 was more of a positional war and did not result in a bloody clash of arms, as did the battle of 1561, for example. This may help explain why it was not included in the Uesugi sources. Having said this, there are several of the above dates that represent nothing more than minor clashes and movements of troops. Of all the confrontations between 1552 and 1564 only the battle in 1561 cost many soldiers their lives. This was perhaps because the military campaigns on the Kawanakajima Plain between 1552 and 1564 were mainly concerned with capturing fortresses and castles in an effort to help their respective lords gain a strategic advantage over one another.

**Illustration 4-21**.

A cavalry soldier attacks. In this scene a samurai on horseback aims for the enemy lines. During the Sengoku Period cavalry soldiers were generally equipped with a *yari* (spear) in addition to the sword. This soldier prepares to strike an enemy at a distance, hence the one-handed grip. He wears a *tatami-gusoku* armor.

The military control Takeda slowly gained over Chikuma has been documented above, but a closer look at the administration of the area is necessary to understand how invading forces maintained the land seized by force. Because the district bordered on the territories of other lords it was used as an important military base, but the resources of the district also had great potential, and Shingen exploited them.

After the Takeda army had incorporated the Chikuma district into Takeda lands, there was obviously a need for a new administration in this newly acquired area. The conquest that had begun in 1548 near the Shiojiri Pass was more or less completed by 1550 when Inukai fort was taken. However, there were still unconquered areas of Chikuma, more specifically the western part of Chikuma, which constituted the other side of the Torii Pass where the Kiso clan lived.

To ensure an effective administration of the Matsumoto area of Chikuma, Shingen first stationed competent generals to ensure the area remained under Takeda control: Baba Nobuharu (1514-1575) was posted as commander at Fukashi Castle in Chikuma, becoming Chikuma district's *bugyô* (magistrate), also called *gundai* (district deputy). Baba had the main responsibility of running the Chikuma district, which entailed everything from military operations to agriculture as well as taking care of the infrastructure. If he turned out to be an ineffective administrator Shingen would soon remove him from the position; on the other hand, if he proved to be successful he would become a very rich and very powerful man.

Hirase Castle, located on the border between the Chikuma and Azumi districts, was attacked and captured by the Takeda army in 1551. Hirase was roughly six kilometers northwest of Fukashi and would now function as a *shijô* (support castle) of Fukashi. A large number of troops were stationed at Hirase, and Shingen posted General Hara Toratane as commander there.

Families that had surrendered without resistance and declared their loyalty to Takeda received letters, called *ando* in Japanese (literally translated as "relief"), confirming the areas they ruled over were still in their possession. These so called *ando* letters often concerned land areas that had belonged to a family for many generations. In some cases their land areas might be increased, while in others decreased. Everything depended on how they reacted to Takeda invasion and their further service under Takeda. Families that had violently opposed the invading force lost all their land to confiscation as a rule. Insurgents were often executed. One example of this practice was the decapitating of 200 members of the Mimura family from the Chikuma district. The land of the Mimura was then portioned out amongst Shingen's men.

Neighbors could also receive a piece of the spoils, especially if they aided the Takeda aggressions. One example of this is the Nakamaki family from the Sarashina district, which borders on Chikuma. Nakamaki Ise *no Kami* was in the service of Baba Nobuharu at Fukashi Castle sometime before 1559, and also served in Baba's Fukashi *zaijô-shû* (stationed castle unit). Nakamaki was rewarded with 15 *kanmon* in 1559, distributed between two villages. The Nakamaki family was a samurai clan of a lower tier; but whatever their status, they had at an early point bowed to the Takeda rule and were rewarded for their loyalty. Baba Nobuharu continued to rule Chikuma from Fukashi Castle up until 1562 (another source states 1560). He was then transferred to Makinoshima Castle in Sarashina.

The choice of a new commander at Fukashi fell on Yamamiya. However, there is some uncertainty concerning the details of this, because it is noted that as early as 1563 Yamamiya was ordered to Wada Castle in Kôzuke together with Atobe Iga *no Kami* and Itagaki Nobuyasu. These three were transferred to Wada Castle's *zaijô-shû*. There is a certain chronological sense in this piece of information, but there are other sources which state that the change of commander took place in 1566. However, the letters of the Yamamiya family support the claim that Yamamiya was commander at Fukashi for a shorter period of time. Therefore there is a gap in the sources concerning the issue of who was commander during the years from 1563 to 1566.

Regardless of which version is correct, after Yamamiya was transferred to Wada a new commander had to be appointed. The choice fell on Kudô Masahide (also known as Naitô Masahide 1523?-1575). It is likely that Masahide became *bugyô*, or *gundai*, of the Chikuma district, but primary sources corroborating this cannot be located; however, the sources confirm he was at least appointed *jôdai* (deputy commander of a castle). Information concerning his position as commander is backed up by a letter dated March 5, 1568. It states that a large restoration project should be commenced at Fukashi, on orders from Shingen. Workers had to be summoned and materials obtained. Repairs and maintenance of fortifications were part of the routine responsibilities of any castle commander, but not all commanders were effective in carrying this work out. It was therefore sometimes necessary to issue direct orders at the highest level, namely from Shingen himself.

In March, 1570 Naitô Masahide (Kudô Masahide) was appointed *jôdai* of Minowa Castle in the Kôzuke province, and Takeda Nobukado was appointed new commander at Fukashi Castle to fill the position. Nobukado did not stay long at Fukashi, because just a year later he was appointed commander at Takatô Castle in the Ina district. Although a new *jôdai* was needed at Fukashi the sources provide little information; and it seems the castle had to do without a commander for some time.

It is most likely that a captain called Minakami Sôfu, who served under Nobukado, stayed on at Fukashi and was finally appointed *jôdai*. The Minakami (may also be read as "Mizukami") family came from the Koma district in Kai and could trace its roots back to the Ogasawara clan. The period between 1571 and 1582 concerning the position of commander at the Fukashi Castle, then, is a little murky. What we have as evidence comes in the form of letters: one letter from 1576 mentions Minakami as *jôdai*. How long Minakami was *jôdai* is uncertain, but it is fully possible that he stayed at Fukashi right up to 1582. However, another source contradicts this assumption, stating instead that when Oda Nagamasu's army attacked Fukashi in February/March 1582 it was Baba Mino *no Kami* who was commander, and who opened the gates of the castle before he fled. The Takeda general Baba Nobuharu was also referred to by his title Mino *no Kami*, but Nobuharu died at Nagashino in 1575, so this cannot refer to him. It is possible Baba Mino was someone from Nobuharu's family and had received the same title by appointment. It would have been quite usual for Baba to inherit the Mino *no Kami* title. Unfortunately there are few sources that refer to the attack on Fukashi Castle in 1582.

Chronology of *jôdai* at Fukashi Castle under Takeda rule:
1550-1562   Baba Nobuharu.
1562-1563   Yamamiya ? (given name unknown).
1563-1570   Naitô Masahide (also known as Kudô Masahide).
1570-1571   Takeda Nobukado.
?-?         Minakami Sôfu.
?-1582      Baba Mino *no Kami* (given name unknown).

In addition to being an administrative and military base, Fukashi also functioned as a kind of prison. Families in the area and districts around Chikuma had to send members of their families as hostages to the Takeda clan to guarantee their loyalty. After a period of time, Takeda gained control over large areas of Shinano, converting other castles for this purpose, but Fukashi was most likely one of the main bases for this type of activity. A letter from 1570 provides proof: at this point the Uesugi clan was a great threat in north Shinano. The hostages mentioned in the letter were members of the Nezu and Tachikawa (also pronounced Tatekawa) families who had first been kept prisoner at Kaizu Castle, on the Kawanakajima Plain. The situation in the area was volatile and the lord of Kaizu decided to send his prisoners to Fukashi, which was further away from the front line.

The Chikuma district was also the area's breadbasket. Shingen treated the district as his personal larder, a kind of storehouse from which he could take out riches and goods, whether they be needed for rewards or maintenance,

without affecting any vassals or increasing taxes. The area was therefore called a *chokkatsu-chi* (area under direct control). However, there is some uncertainty concerning how cavalier Shingen was in his treatment of Chikuma's resources, as there are few sources that support the theories concerning the so-called *chokkatsu-chi* area in Chikuma.

How much power and what sort of role did the Fukashi Castle's *jôdai* have?

- Naturally enough the lord of Fukashi had authority over the castle's *zaijô-shû* (soldiers stationed at castle), and could dispatch troops to engage in various operations within his district, such as guard duty, policing duties, escort missions, and also to quell any small *Ikki* rebellions.
- Fukashi Castle functioned as a storehouse for food and supplies awaiting transport to other parts of the Takeda family's territories. It was the Fukashi lord's responsibility to make sure all this ran smoothly.
- When farmers or *ji-samurai* were called up for military service they were asked to gather at Fukashi Castle at a certain date. As a rule, those called up had to take along weapons and other equipment; some of the fortresses, though, had weapons and armor, which could be loaned to soldiers for the period of a campaign. Whether Fukashi Castle had such a store of such equipment is not known, but it seems likely.
- The commander functioned as a link between the central administration in Tsutsujigasaki in Kai and the local families in Chikuma. Complaints or requests from families in Chikuma were handed over to the lord of Fukashi, who then passed them on to Shingen in Kai if necessary. Evidence suggests that letters from Shingen to families in the Chikuma district also went via the lord at Fukashi, although the letters' contents wouldn't necessarily concern the commander.
- The commander and his staff at Fukashi also functioned as a kind of group of teachers/supervisors for the *jitô* class of local officials in the Chikuma district.

Eventually, Fukashi received a new name in or around 1582, and from that time is known as Matsumoto Castle. It became an administrative center for families such as Ogasawara, Ishikawa, Toda, Matsudaira, Horita, and Mizuno. Until 1867 Matsumoto (Fukashi) Castle functioned as a main headquarters for the administrator (*gundai*) of Chikuma.

The whole of the central Honshû Island shook in its collective boots when the words *Takeda kibatai* (Takeda cavalry) were uttered - at least this is the usual belief among students of the Takeda clan. But is there any truth to this, or is the ability of the legendary Takeda cavalry a well established myth? A myth that has grown in strength in the fertile soil of the more recent sources from the end of the 1800s and beginning of the 1900s. The sources and books from this period give the impression that the Takeda cavalry wreaked havoc on the battlefields over a period of decades in the 1500s, and it was only when *teppô* were first used in large numbers in mid-1570s that the Takeda cavalry began to suffer defeats.

The cavalry ensured victory on many occasions, but ironically it was not always on horseback. The Japanese landscape was not always suited to large-scale use of mounted cavalry attacks. As we have seen so far in this book many of the armed conflicts involved the storming and capturing of castles and fortresses. In this type of conflict mounted cavalry was of limited effectiveness. However, during these kind of attacks cavalry soldiers would often be on foot, but were skilful warriors whether or not they were mounted on horseback.

Nevertheless, it is the picture of a samurai on horseback that we associate with the Takeda clan. But were they really as impressive as we are led to believe from the sources and books of more recent times? If we steer clear of the so-called short stories and the partly unreliable sources of the Edo Period, not to mention samurai films made in the twentieth century, then it is clear that the expression *Takeda kibatai* starts to show cracks, indeed large cracks. In what follows we will consider more closely the Takeda clan's cavalry forces and the legendary Takeda horses.

**Photo TAK 4-48 (top left), TAK 4-49 (top right), TAK 4-50 (bottom left)**

Three photos of the Kiso horse. Short legs, round belly, and a short thick neck are the typical features of the Kiso horse. These would be the horses the samurai used during the Middle Ages of Japan. (Kaida village, Kiso Fukushima, Nagano prefecture)

**Photo TAK 4-51 (bottom right)**

A Japanese man next to a Kiso horse. The person in the picture is about 160cm tall, near the average height of a samurai during the 16th century. This photo shows us what the Japanese horse looked like during the Sengoku Period. (Kaida village, Kiso Fukushima, Nagano prefecture)

Before Japanese horses had samurai on their backs they had been used through the centuries as workhorses in the thousands of villages throughout the numerous islands which make up Japan. They were used in the paddy fields, to clear forests, haul timber, transport goods, etc. These abilities could also be exploited for military activities. So although the horses were gradually taken into use by the military they were first there to help the common farmer in the running of his farm.

According to the sources, the origins of the Takeda cavalry as a military unit reach as far back as the Genpei war (1180-1185). The reputation of the family's military cavalry division spread far and wide even then. Horses of high quality were bred through the centuries, especially horses of great stamina and strength, although the horses were not especially large. The horses were very much in demand and could be purchased, for example, as gifts. Every year since the Heian Period (782-1181), the Kai province provided roughly sixty horses for the emperor and his court in Kyôto. The best breeding grounds for the horses were the three large plains of the Kai province: Kashiwazaki, Makino, and Hosaka. Families living in these areas, such as the Amari family in the Koma district in Kai, were often horse breeders. By means of letters the Takeda clan would make their horse needs known. Horses were also bred in other areas, such as Ogasawara-*maki*, Hemi-*maki*, Iino-*maki*, Iwami-*maki*, and Hatta-*maki* (*maki* means "a meadow"). These areas most likely belonged to the Ogasawara, Hemi, Iino, Iwami, and Hatta families, thereby explaining the names of the plains.

As mentioned there were three main areas in Kai; two of these, Kashiwazaki and Makino, were inside the northern Koma district, while the Hosaka area lay a little to the south, near present-day Nirasaki town. All three plains are situated in the area between Yatsuga-take Mountain and the southern mountains - in other words, in the northwest of Kai province.

At an early age, the boys of a samurai clan were introduced to horses. A young samurai spent a lot of his time on horseback, learning to control the animal and getting to know it well enough that horse and rider were in harmony. As part of the training long riding trips were daily fare with various hindrances, such as rivers, hills, and mountains. In addition to being a first-rate rider, the young samurai also had to learn to fight on horseback, and his equestrian training included training in fighting from horseback with various weapons.

Up until the Sengoku Period a cavalry samurai was primarily an archer, part of a kind of mobile artillery unit. In addition to the bow he also carried a *tachi* (sword) and, usually, a *tantô* (dagger) on his hip. At the start of a battle, the cavalry would ride towards the enemy and shoot their arrows, then return to their own ranks. Of course, the samurai soldier was also trained to use the sword, spear, and *naginata* and never avoided a good fight at close quarters if he could help it. More often than not this kind of man-to-man confrontation characterized the end of battles, usually on foot rather than horseback.

Such was the situation for the cavalry for several hundred years, but in the 1500s the infantry had taken over the role as archers, and from that time onwards the cavalry were mostly equipped with spears. The spear in fact became their main weapon, but they would always carry a sword as well. The spear they used was roughly 2 to 2.5 meters long and was known as the *bajô-yari* (cavalry spear), *inu-yari* (dog spear), or by other names. The spears were much shorter than those carried by the infantry. Spear lengths could also vary significantly from clan to clan, and from soldier to soldier. One reason why the cavalry's spears were so short in relation to the infantryman's spear is that the horses they rode were small of stature compared to modern day horses and the samurai soldier would also hold the spear in both hands to use it to full effect. A long spear of roughly 4 to 5 meters would probably have been quite cumbersome to use.

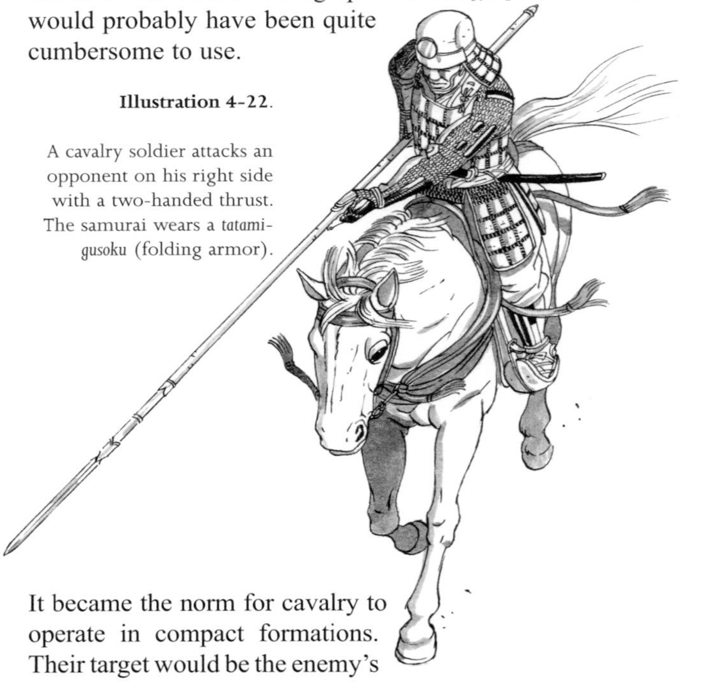

**Illustration 4-22.**

A cavalry soldier attacks an opponent on his right side with a two-handed thrust. The samurai wears a *tatami-gusoku* (folding armor).

It became the norm for cavalry to operate in compact formations. Their target would be the enemy's cavalry or infantry divisions. They would seek weak points in the enemy's ranks and attempt to break them up. These attacking formations would often end up in straightforward man-to-man confrontations with the enemy's cavalry. In addition to spears, some cavalry troops also chose to use the fearsome *naginata* or *nagamaki* weapons. In the hands of a skilful cavalryman these weapons were deadly, and an infantryman would be wise to flee if he saw a mounted samurai approaching wielding one. Standing in the stirrups of his horse the cavalryman would swing his *naginata* from one side to the other in large arcs, hacking down anything that stood in his way. Such a weapon could almost effortlessly slice a person in two, even if the person in question was wearing armor. The *nagamaki* weapon could also be used in the same way; its shaft and blade were more or less of equal length, and it was used as a type of long sword. On the battlefield a foot soldier's life hung from a thin thread if they happened to be near a cavalryman when he came swinging something like that.

**Illustration 4-23.**

A cavalry soldier attacks, he is aiming his spear on a foot soldier on his left side. He wears a *tatami-gusoku* armor.

**Photo TAK 4-52**

Japanese horseshoes. It was not until the mid-19th century that iron shoes for horses came to Japan. Before this import horseshoes made of straw were used. (Courtesy of the Uma no Hakubutsukan, Yokohama city)

The use of the spear often involved holding the spear in the right hand and jabbing against the enemy on the right side of the horse. If a cavalryman approached him on his left side the left hand would be used as support on the spearshaft. The cavalryman could also swing his spear over his head like a fan, a technique often used against infantry formations to keep the enemy at bay, and try to create fear/panic. A mounted samurai could also throw his spear and then draw his sword; but on the whole, the spear was used as a type of lance.

*Teppô* (matchlock guns) were introduced and used in considerable numbers during the second half of the sixteenth century, reducing the role of the cavalry on the open battlefield to a secondary one. But *teppô* weren't the only thing which reduced the role of the cavalry. Large divisions of spear infantry armed with spears sometimes exceeding six meters (the length could vary from clan to clan) meant that mounted samurai could be kept at a distance. The role of the cavalry had now changed and was mainly concerned with keeping the cavalry of the opposing force at bay, and tracking down beaten enemies on the battlefield - a kind of clearing action. The cavalry seldom played a prominent or decisive role in the battles of the sixteenth century.

The question has in fact been raised of whether the cavalry played a prominent role at any time in Japanese history. Recent re-examination of old sources provides us with little information suggesting there were a large number of occasions when the cavalry played a prominent role. Japanese horses were small, and, in addition, their horseshoes were made of straw (*wara no kutsu*). The type of horseshoe used is of great importance in determining how well a horse functions, whether it be a military horse or a work-horse. Horseshoes of metal were not introduced into Japan until the mid nineteenth century. The consequence, then, of using straw horseshoes was that a horse's hooves were vulnerable to a myriad of problems and were unable to accomplish the same workload as a horse with metal horseshoes. Campaigns which lasted a long time and went over long distances must have worn down the horses to a great extent. It is very likely that an army during this period required a large number of extra horses when going on extended campaigns.

Another unique aspect of the Japanese military horse, or more specifically, the equipment they carried was the stirrups. They were called *abumi* and were completely different from what was used in the west. However, old burial finds reveal they initially bore a close resemblance to those used in the west. Called *wa-abumi* in Japanese (which means something like 'ring stirrups'), they were very simple in form and almost completely round. During the Nara and Heian Period (710-1185) the stirrup gradually took on its characteristic appearance as used by the samurai from the Genpei Period and right up to the mid-19th century. There may be several reasons to explain why stirrups in Japan gradually came to be formed as they were; but one must have been that since it was completely open a rider who fell from his horse would not get his foot caught in the stirrup. This was often a problem in the west, where cavalrymen are known to have died from the injuries they sustained after being dragged behind a horse with their foot caught in the stirrup.

Another factor was the *waraji* (straw sandals) mounted samurai wore on their feet. These straw sandals offered no protection from weapons in combat. Because of the unusual arc shape of the Japanese stirrups, the toes on the foot were now completely protected, and one could also use the stirrup as a weapon. The stirrup itself was made of iron or wood and painted in black or red color, but other colors with patterns were also used. Examples of wooden stirrups exist dating all the way back to the Kamakura Period. With the new stirrup it was possible for a mounted

**Illustration 4-24.**

Various stirrups used in Japan from ancient times up to the 19th century. The earliest stirrup used in Japan was the same as the one used in China. Then sometime around the Heian Period changes to the Japanese stirrup came about. Exactly why these changes took place is unknown, but it might have something to do with samurai footwear and the way the stirrup, with the changes, could now be used as a weapon. From top to bottom: ancient period stirrup found in burial mounds; Nara Period (710-784); Heian Period (794-1185); 15th century, used throughout the Sengoku and Edo Periods. The stirrup used during the Kamakura Period (1185-1336) resembles the one used during the 15th century. The samurai in the illustration is using the Kamakura period stirrup.

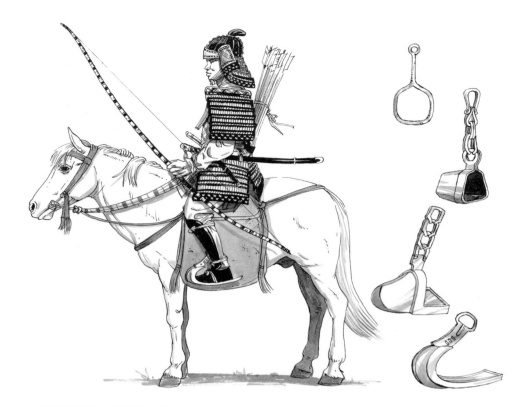

**Photo TAK 4-53 (left) & TAK 4-54 (bottom)**

The Japanese *abumi* (stirrups). (Courtesy of the Uma no Hakubutsukan, Yokohama city)

samurai to kick a foot soldier down without breaking his toes. A kick to the head with this new stirrup could be lethal.

Although the cavalry in the sixteenth century no longer played a leading role on the battlefield, the number of horses nevertheless increased greatly. The reason for this increase was undoubtedly the enormous armies formed during this century; a large number of soldiers needed a lot of supplies, and often quickly. The main form of transportation was the horse, which carried everything on its back. Military campaigns in the second half of the sixteenth century went from being strictly local affairs, lasting a few days or a week, to campaigns that could go on for several weeks or even months, often in a neighboring province. The lords finally became aware of the resources such operations demanded, and one of the measures adopted was to intensify horse-breeding. Suddenly there was an acute need for supply horses and provinces such as Kai and Shinano began to prosper in this trade.

There is little information available for the period around 1550 concerning the ratio of cavalry to infantry in the Takeda clan, but references here and there provide some indication of how many cavalrymen the Takeda clan had. For instance, one source states that the Takeda clan fought in a battle with 3,000 cavalry, but another source states 3,000 men. Although the sources refer to the same campaign, nothing clarifies

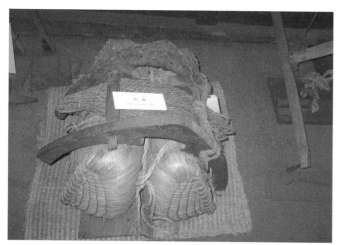

Photo TAK 4-55

A *nigura* (packhorse saddle). During the Sengoku Period thousands of horses with this type of saddle were used to carry all kinds of goods across Japan. (Courtesy of the Uma no Hakubutsukan, Yokohama City)

whether the number concerned were only cavalrymen or just infantrymen, or a combination of the two.

A more recent analysis of the relative strength of the Takeda army when they invaded Suwa in the 1540s proposes the following explanation. Shingen is said to have mobilized as many as 30,000 men, of which 3,000 were cavalrymen, or 10% of the army on horseback. If we consider the contemporary sources, only one reference from 1542 mentions such large numbers of infantrymen in relation to cavalry. It is impossible to say whether this figure is correct because of the dearth of available sources. The above information makes it difficult to give definite and credible figures for how many cavalrymen the Takeda clan had at their disposal before 1550. After 1550 *Kôyô gunkan* is more or less the only source that provides us with reasonably detailed information concerning the number of cavalry.

However, a number of irregularities have been pointed out in the *Kôyô gunkan* source, and these are also valid concerning the information dealing with the Takeda clan's military organization. An example of this is the reference that Kôsaka Danjô Masanobu is said to have been in command of over 450 cavalry, and that Obata Nobusada is said to have led 500 cavalry, i.e. samurai who are under his direct control (his vassals). It is possible that a number of cavalrymen were placed with the generals who were at the top of the list, the veterans, and that they therefore cannot be called house vassals under the general they served. The reason for the skepticism concerning this information is that the person said to have written *Kôyô gunkan*, Obata Kagenori, was most likely a relation of Obata Nobusada, and Kagenori has possibly exaggerated Nobusada's figures somewhat. Not only that, if the figure of 500 cavalry is correct, then Obata must have been one of the richest generals in Kai, because it was very costly

to mobilize cavalry. To compare, then, the sources from 1575 show that the Uesugi clan in Echigo had 5,503 armed men and 566 of these were cavalry. If one compares these figures then the reference of about 500 cavalry for Obata seems very high. Also concerning Kôsaka Danjô there is also a suspicious link to *Kôyô gunkan*. It is said in fact that Obata Kagenori was not the main author of *Kôyô gunkan*, but instead one of Shingen's generals, namely Kôsaka Danjô Masanobu, is rumored to have written the first books of the source collection. It is because of this connection that there are doubts about the number of cavalry it reports as being under Kôsaka's command.

Here follows an overview of the cavalry forces which the various generals of the Takeda clan had at their disposition, according to the source *Kôyô gunkan*:

*Fudai - Karô-shû* (inner vassals - senior vassals)

| | |
|---|---|
| Akiyama Nobutomo - | 50 cavalry |
| Baba Nobuharu - | 120 cavalry |
| Komiyama Masatomo - | 30 cavalry |
| Yamagata Masakage - | 300 cavalry |
| Komai Masanao - | 55 cavalry |
| Oyamada Nobushige - | 200 cavalry |
| Kôsaka Masanobu - | 450 cavalry |
| Naitô Masatoyo - | 250 cavalry |
| Kurihara Akifuyu - | 100 cavalry |
| Imafuku Jôkan - | 70 cavalry |
| Atobe Katsusuke - | 300 cavalry |
| Asari Nobutane - | 120 cavalry |
| Amari Masatada - | 100 cavalry |
| Hara Masatane - | 120 cavalry |
| Oyamada Masayuki - | 70 cavalry |
| Tsuchiya Masatsugu - | 100 cavalry |
| Atobe Katsutada - | 50 cavalry |

*Go-Shinrui-shû* (family members)

| | |
|---|---|
| Takeda Nobutoyo - | 200 cavalry |
| Takeda Nobukado - | 80 cavalry |
| Takeda Katsuyori - | 200 cavalry |
| Ichijô Nobutatsu - | 200 cavalry |
| Kawakubo Nobuzane - | 15 cavalry |
| Takeda Saemon - | 100 cavalry |
| Nishina Morinobu - | 100 cavalry |
| Mochizuki Masayori - | 60 cavalry |
| Katsurayama Nobusada - | 120 cavalry |
| Itagaki Nobuyasu - | 120 cavalry |
| Kiso Yoshimasa - | 200 cavalry |
| Anayama Nobukimi - | 200 cavalry |

This is not a complete list as far as the Takeda clan's organization as listed in the *Kôyô gunkan*, but it shows the content of the groups *Shinrui-shû* and *Fudai/Karô-shû*.

A percentage rule, which is often used for the sixteenth century, is that 10% to 15% of a military unit consisted of cavalry; this is born out by contemporary sources. As far as the Takeda clan is concerned, the figure may be somewhat higher. If one considers the source *Kôyô gunkan* then the percent figure is impossible to calculate, because there are no figures for the infantry soldiers, although we have figures for cavalry. According to *Kôyô gunkan,* then, the Takeda had at their disposition 9,340 cavalry. As already mentioned, there are many critical voices concerning the exactness of the *Kôyô gunkan*, and more recent research and analyses of the source material from the middle of the sixteenth century provide us with evidence that the Takeda clan also had roughly 10% cavalry. But an important point here is the issue of which period the calculations were made in. It is important to keep in mind that as Shingen conquered more and more land, so too did his army grow in size. More soldiers could be called up for war service from the newly acquired areas of land. Therefore it is certain that Shingen had a large percentage of cavalry in his army, but there are few who would believe that this was higher than twenty percent. A new theory presented calculates roughly 50,000 armed soldiers for Takeda, at its greatest extent, and of these 9,340 were cavalry, or roughly one in five was a cavalryman This does not seem an unrealistic figure if we consider the calculation for 1570. At this time Shingen ruled over several provinces and was then one of the most powerful lords in the eastern part of Honshû.

Another analysis of a more recent date considers the relative strength of the Takeda clan's army and divides up a troop of 100 men in the following manner: 12 cavalry, 58 soldiers with spears, 7 with *teppô*, 10 archers, 6 flag bearers, and 7 others. The 7 'others' were most likely *ashigaru* with various non-combatant roles, but it was also expected that these soldiers should bear arms if necessary. The year and date which provides the basis for these calculations is not referred to, but it was most likely towards the end of the 1560s.

Shingen developed the infrastructure in Kai and built better and more roads. He did this to increase the mobility of his army. When the alarm from a *noroshi-dai* was given at the border, Shingen could mobilize his men, dispatching his cavalry and foot soldiers quickly against the enemy. It was important to confront the enemy as quickly as possible, so that they would have little time to wreak havoc inside the province.

In addition to playing the role of warhorse, horses were also used to transport all kinds of supplies. This crucial role is often forgotten, but the success of a military campaign depended on maintaining solid lines of supply. Here the Takeda clan was also first with a new practice: every Takeda campaign included a large *konida-tai* (supply train). This division made sure that the army was supplied with food and equipment and was led by a general with *bugyô* status.

The horse and wagon was not used much in Japan. The topography and the type of roads explain this: high mountain chains and narrow paths were not suited to wagons. However, the roads were good enough to use packhorses in large numbers.

Photo TAK 4-56

A packhorse. During a military campaign there were hundreds and even thousands of these horses in use. The Takeda were fortunate to have a large production of horses in Kai and later on also in Shinano. Note the *waraji* (shoes) on its hooves. (Courtesy of the Nagano kenritsu rekishikan).

The availability of a large number of horses was a blessing for the Takeda clan. A samurai cavalryman most likely had with him one or two extra horses when he was on a campaign. This was necessary, because during a battle there was a great risk of injury to the horses. Horses were also used to transport soldiers to the battle zone; cavalry soldiers would often dismount from their horses and become foot soldiers once they reached the front line, for instance in the case of sieges. But once hostilities had ceased they would need the horses to return home again.

When did horses first come to Kai and where did they come from? It is believed the horses originated in China and Korea, but some experts argue there have been horses in Japan for thousands of years, as far back as the Jômon period (1,000 BC) and beyond. This might be true, but still other voices argue that the first horses might have crossed over from Alaska during the ice age. With scarce archaeological evidence to verify any of these theories this debate will not easily be resolved. Regardless of where Japanese horses originated from written evidence does support a great number of horses were brought to Japan from Korea. This also seems likely, as Korea was Japan's nearest cultural neighbor. The Mongolian invasions in 1274 and 1281 are also said to have brought horses to Japan, but these horses most likely remained on the southern island of Kyûshû and did not much influence the breeds of horses further east in the country. The Mongols' horses are also said to have been quite small and were most likely very few in number.

Just as the question of when horses were introduced in Japan is cloudy, so too is the riddle of when they first made their appearance in Kai lost to history. Excavations in recent years have provided the earliest finds of horse teeth in Kai dating back to the fourth century, proving that these horses were used at that time in Kai.

Three main breeds of horses existed in Japan during this time: Kiso, Misaki, and Dosanko. The latter are to be found on the island of Hokkaidô. As far as the Kiso breed is concerned, it was kept in the Shinano province, but did spread to neighboring areas, among them the Kai province. There were also other breeds such as the Noma from Ehime prefecture, Taishûba (also called Tsushima horse, from the island of the same name between Korea and Japan), Tokara from Kagoshima prefecture, Miyako from Okinawa and the breed Yonakuni. What is common for all the breeds that have existed, and those that still exist, is that they were relatively small of stature. The horse kept and bred in Kai was called *Kurokoma* (the black horse).

Recent excavations have provided important clues concerning the size and weight of the samurai horses of the sixteenth century. The results of the excavations from a 1333 battlefield show that the horses found were between 109cm and 140cm high. These excavations also provide us with indications of several horse breeds in Japan at the time. In excavations made near Tsutsujigasaki Estate in Kôfu in 1989, a horse was found which was roughly twelve years old and estimated to be roughly 120cm tall. This and other finds, then, have provided researchers with enough information to enable them to calculate what the average horse looked like in sixteenth century Japan.

In addition to excavations in recent times, written records give us some references to the height of the horses in Medieval Japan. Among these are the *Agatsumakagami* and the *Taihei-ki* sources. In these two we find specific horses with heights between 140cm and 145cm that belonged to famous lords. These were most likely exceptions to the average height of 130cm. One could say that the highest rank samurai kept the best horse for himself – this is probably a correct assumption.

A Sengoku Period (1467-1615) horse probably weighed between 250kg and 350kg, and measured between 120cm and 130cm to

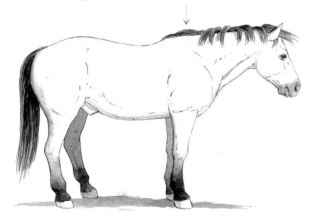

**Illustration 4-25.**

A typical horse from 16<sup>th</sup> century Japan. The illustration is based on a photograph of a Kiso horse. The average horse's height was 130 centimeters, measured at the horse's shoulders (see the arrow). Short legs, round belly, and a short thick neck were all characteristics of a Japanese horse from the Middle Ages.

the horse's back. A samurai at that time was on average roughly 157cm tall and weighed, including armor, roughly 75kg. If we compare the samurai horses to present day horses, then 130cm is not much of an impressive sight. For comparison, present-day thoroughbred horses measure between 160cm to 175cm high and weigh approximately 500kg.

The importation of horses towards the end of the nineteenth century meant that Japanese horse breeds experienced a considerable decrease in numbers with the new larger breeds becoming more dominant. Before and during the Second World War Japan used an enormous number of horses in warfare, especially in China. It might be said that during the period from 1931 to 1945 the original horse breeds of Japan received their deathblow. Nowadays, original Japanese breeds are few in number. The number of original Japanese horses still in Japan were taken from an investigation carried out between 2001 and 2002. Of the breed Dosanko, 1,857 remain; of the Kiso breed, 136 are all that is left; and only 120 of the once-numerous Misaki breed remain. All are still of small stature and weigh between 250kg and 350kg.

As far as speed is concerned the Kiso breed from the Shinano province has been clocked at 39.4 kph. If one puts a cavalry soldier equipped in armor on the horse's back, then recent measurements show that the horses would quickly have run out of steam.

So the question may be asked about the extent to which the find of one horse at Tsutsujigasaki reflects the average horse that the Takeda clan used at that time? The question is whether the idea we have of the impressive cavalry divisions of the Takeda clan needs to be re-evaluated somewhat, because very strong evidence exists that the horses the Takeda used were no taller than 120cm to 140cm. However, one can probably assume that the average height of the horses from Kai was at least 140cm. This is because books which deal with horse breeding in the Kai province, always stated the horses from Kai were a very attractive breed, known for their stamina and speed, and one cannot take that away from them. The horses in Japan, then, were very strong and robust, but also small. As a point of interest, Oda Nobunaga is said to have had a horse measuring as much as 150cm. This piece of information shows us some horses stood out from the rest. Yet, what seems to contradict the fact that the horses in Kai were any larger than average is precisely the find at Tsutsujigasaki, of an unimpressive specimen of horse measuring only 120cm. Seen through today's eyes, then, the samurai 'horse' must be changed to 'pony,' if one is to best explain what the Takeda cavalry used in sixteenth century Japan. The image we have in our minds of a proud samurai on his large and powerful horse is one that unfortunately has been portrayed and reinforced through films and books over the last hundred years, one that does not accurately reflect the historical reality.

After a battle the injured had to be treated in the best way possible. The majority of clans kept a doctor or a group of doctors in their service and the Takeda clan was by no means an exception to the rule. Throughout his time as leader of the Takeda Shingen was concerned about the welfare and treatment of his injured soldiers.

Shingen made sure camp doctors followed the campaigns and stood ready to treat the injured both during and after a battle. According to *Kôyô gunkan* Shingen had three doctors in his service: Itasaka Hôin Munetaka, Itasaka Bokusai, and Yamamoto Dairin. A fourth person called Mishuku Kenmotsu is said to have also practiced as a doctor in Shingen's medical units. According to one source, Bokusai was only a young boy at the time, reputed to be a son of Hôin; it does not seem that he practiced at the same time as the others. However, if he was the son of Hôin, then he probably followed in his father's footsteps, although some historians believe there is no proof that Hôin and Bokusai were related. The three doctors officially mentioned were said to have belonged to Shingen's *Otogi-shû* (advisory group). Itasaka Hôin is said to have initially served the *Shôgun* in Kyôto, but the unrest in the capital worried him and he traveled to Etchû only to encounter *Ikkô Ikki* wreaking havoc, so he chose to journey further. He finally reached Kai, where he went into Shingen's service. Bokusai was a Buddhist priest who initially resided at the Nanzenji temple in Kyôto and who moved to Kai in response to a request from Shingen. These three doctors were all important persons to the clan and were always on call to help Shingen in the event of a crisis. Which one of the three was Shingen's personal doctor is unclear, but it is possible that all three were.

On the battlefield, at least one of these three main doctors, along with several aides, was in attendance. The aides could be anything from samurai to *ashigaru* charged with helping comrades in need. Unfortunately, during this period in Japan medical science was limited to little more than basic first aid such as binding sores and cuts. This could involve extracting arrows from the various parts of the injured soldier's body. These operations were often carried out by skilled medical personnel - for example the field doctor, if he was available – whenever possible. Too often though, soldier comrades carried out such operations and although they struggled to protect wounds many injured died from infections in the aftermath of a military campaign.

Just as the study of medicine and medical science came from China, so the first doctors probably did as well. Initially they were mainly to be found serving the emperor and the nobility in Kyôto. During the Sengoku Period it seems the medical profession had spread to several parts of Japan. However, the majority of doctors still practiced their profession in Kyôto. In Shingen's case, it was he who persuaded doctors from Kyôto to serve in Kai, so he was able to build a medical team to serve the Takeda clan. Before the science of treating the injured became widespread in Japan there were persons in the clan interested in medicine who would act as doctors. This often involved utilizing the practical experience they had gained from numerous campaigns which resulted in a kind of practical knowledge, but at a limited level.

## ONSEN

Shingen was also very much interested in the rehabilitation of his injured soldiers. He established rehabilitation centers near beneficial hot springs *(onsen)* from which the centers gained their name in and around Kai and Shinano provinces. Evidence exists of the Takeda soldiers' use of these *onsen* areas from various contemporary letters preserved at the Erinji temple in Enzan town.

Every *onsen* developed included buildings for guests, storage, and servant quarters. Shingen was himself also a frequent user of the *onsen*. According to the source *Kôyô gunkan*, after being injured at Uedahara in 1548, Shingen stayed roughly thirty days at Shima-no-yu (Yumura *onsen*) to heal his wounds.

There were also people in service who nursed the sick and injured at these places of rehabilitation. In addition to the use of pure spring water for the treatment of tired and injured soldiers, various plants and herbs were also used to heal wounds. It is likely these medicines originated from China, where they had already been in use for centuries This branch of medical science is still widely recognized today throughout the world.

According to the sources, we find the Yumura *onsen*, Kawaura *onsen*, and the Shimobe *onsen* among the most important in Kai at that time. Each of these rehabilitation centers was used for the treatment of injured soldiers. Other *onsen* were probably used to rehabilitate soldiers (namely: Sekisuiji *onsen*, Tano *onsen*, Sagashio *onsen*, and Masutomi *onsen*). In Shinano it was primarily the *onsen* areas in the Suwa district that were used. Before Shingen's army set off on a campaign many of these *onsen* were ordered to make preparations for a large admittance of injured soldiers when the military campaign was over. The *onsen* were also used for pure recreation and became important meeting places for the soldiers.

*Bigman special - Takeda Shingen.* Sekaibunkasha Tokyo, 1994.
*Buki to Bôgu Nihonhen.* By Toda Tôsei, Shinkigensha 1998.
*Imagawa-shi no kenkyû.* By Owada Tetsuo, Seibunsha 2000.
*Imagawa Yoshimoto no subete.* Shinjinbutsu ôraisha 1994.
*Kai Takeda-shi.* By Ueno Haruo, Shinjinbutsu ôraisha 1972.
*Kanagawa-ken no rekishi - kenshi 14.* Yamakawa shuppansha 2001 (f. 1996).
*Kôfu shishi shiryôhen 1 genshi kodai chûsei.* Kôfu-shi yakusho, Gyôsei 1989.
*Komoro shishi rekishihen 2.* Komoro 1984.
*Kôyô gunkan 1,2 and 3.* Translated by Koshihara Tetsurô, Kyôikusha 1979.
*Matsumoto-jô - meijô series 5.* Gakken 1995.
*Meishô Takeda Shingen.* Takeda jinja Kôfu 1988.
*Nagano-ken no rekishi - kenshi 20.* Yamakawa shuppansha Tokyo 1997.
*Nihon kassen zuten.* By Sasama Yoshihiko, Yûsankaku 1997.
*Nihon no kassen bugu jiten.* By Sasama Yoshihiko, Kashiwa shobô 1999.
*Nihon no meizoku 5.* Shinjinbutsu ôraisha Tokyo 1989.
*Nihon no rekishi 11 Sengoku daimyô.* Chûkô bunko 1976.
*Rekishi dokuhon 5 Meishô Takeda Shingen.* Shinjinbutsu ôraisha 1987.
*Rekishi dokuhon Sengoku no jô - jissen data file.* Shinjinbutsu ôraisha 1995.
*Rekishi dokuhon special 44.* Shinjinbutsu ôraisha 1993.
*Rekishi dokuhon special 52.* Shinjinbutsu ôraisha 1995.
*Rekishi dokuhon 5 Takeda Shingen.* Shinjinbutsu ôraisha 1969.
*Rekishi gunzô selection - Uesugi Kenshin.* Gakken Tokyo 2001.
*Rekishi gunzô series - 2, 5, 6, 7, 8, 13, 50.* Gakken Tokyo 1988 -1997.
*Rekishi gunzô visual kassen series 3 - Sengoku no tatakai.* Gakken Tokyo 1996.
*Rekishi to tabi Sengoku dôran 135 no tatakai.* Akita shoten Tokyo 1996.
*Rekishi to tabi 1 Gekitotsu Kawanakajima no kassen.* Akita shoten Tokyo 1982.
*Rekishi to tabi 1 Kai no tora Takeda Shingen.* Akita shoten Tokyo 1987.
*Rekishi to tabi 6 Sengoku bushô to senryaku shûdan.* Akita shoten Tokyo 1988.
*Rekishi to tabi 10 Sengoku rakujô monogatari.* Akita shoten Tokyo 1978.
*Rekishi to tabi 10 Sengoku saikyô Takeda gundan.* Akita shoten Tokyo 1980.
*Rekishi to tabi 9 Takeda Shingen jôraku daisakusen.* Akita shoten Tokyo 1988.
*Rekishi to tabi Takeda Shingen sôran.* Akita shoten Tokyo 1985.
*Rekishi to tabi zusetsu Takeda Shingen no sekai.* Akita shoten Tokyo 1988.

*Sakaki chôshi chû rekishihen.* Sakaki 1981.
*Sengoku bushô monoshiri jiten.* Shufu to seikatsusha Tokyo 1992.
*Sengoku bushô senryaku senjutsu jiten.* Shufu to seikatsusha 1994.
*Sengoku bushô - Takeda Shingen.* Shinjinbutsu ôraisha 1988.
*Sengoku daimyô keifu jinmei jiten - tôkoku hen.* Shinjinbutsu ôraisha 1985.
*Sengoku daimyô no nichijô seikatsu.* By Sasamoto Shôji, Kodansha sensho 2000.
*Sengoku daimyô Takeda-shi no kenkyû.* By Sasamoto Shôji, Shibunkaku shuppan 1993.
*Sengoku jinmei jiten.* Shinjinbutsu ôraisha 1997.
*Sengoku kassen daijiten 3.* Shinjinbutsu ôraisha 1989.
*Sengoku kassen manual.* By Tôgô Ryû, Kodansha 2001.
*Sengoku Takeda no jô.* By Nakada Masamitsu, Yûhô shoten shinsha 1988.
*Shizuoka-ken no rekishi - kenshi 22.* Yamakawa shuppansha 1998.
*Takeda bushi no keifu.* By Dobashi Jijû, Shinjinbutsu ôraisha 1972.
*Takeda ichizoku no subete.* Shinjinbutsu ôraisha 1998.
*Takeda-shi kenkyû 15.* Iwata shoin, Tokyo 1995.
*Takeda-shi kenkyû 21.* Iwata shoin, Tokyo 1999.
*Takeda Shingen.* By Okuno Takahiro, Yoshikawa kobunkan 1987.
*Takeda Shingen.* By Sasamoto Shôji, Chûkô shinsho 1997.
*Takeda Shingen daijiten.* Shinjinbutsu ôraisha 2000.
*Takeda Shingen ha doko kara kita ka.* By Iwasaki Seigo, Yamanashi furusato bunko 1996.
*Takeda Shingen kassen-ki.* By Sakamoto Tokuichi, Shinjinbutsu ôraisha 1975.
*Takeda Shingen magoko no senpô.* By Sakamoto Tokuichi, Shinjinbutsu ôraisha 1987.
*Takeda Shingen nazo no gunbai.* By Baba Noriaki, Shinjinbutsu ôraisha 2000.
*Takeda Shingen no subete.* Shinjinbutsu ôraisha 1978.
*Takeda Shingen omoshiro jiten.* By Hasegawa Tatsuo, Shinjinbutsu ôraisha 1987.
*Takeda Shingen sono karei naru keifu.* By Sakamoto Tokuichi, Akita shoten 1988.
*Takeda Shingen to Suwa.* Suwa shidankai 1974.
*Takeda-shi no Shinano shihai.* By Sasamoto Shôji, Meichô shuppan Tokyo 1990.
*Tanbô Nihon no jô 4 Nakasendô.* Shôgakkan 1978.
*Teihon Kai hyakuji.* Kyôdo shuppansha 1996.
*Teihon Takeda Shingen.* By Isogai Masayoshi, Shinjinbutsu ôraisha 1982.
*Teppô-tai to kiba gundan.* By Suzuki Masaya, Yôsensha 2003.
*Uesugi Kenshin jôraku no nazo.* By Baba Noriaki, Kindai bungeisha 1997.
*Yamanashi-ken no rekishi - kenshi 19.* Yamakawa shuppansha 1999.
*Zukai Sengoku kassen 50.* Shinjinbutsu ôraisha 2003.

# AVAILABLE TITLES IN THE SAGA OF THE SAMURAI SERIES

*Saga of the Samurai: Book 1*

## TAKEDA RISES TO POWER
### THE KAI TAKEDA 1 (1130-1467)

Book 1 in this series explores the beginning and early history of the Takeda family of Kai Province, including the political and military struggle of the clan to maintain its influence. This thrilling tale spans over 500 years of Japanese history from the Takeda clan's point of view.

*Saga of the Samurai: Book 2*

## TAKEDA NOBUTORA: THE UNIFICATION OF KAI
### THE KAI TAKEDA 2 (1494-1574)

Book 2 in this series focuses on the life of Takeda Nobutora (1494-1574), father to Takeda Shingen. Nobutora's life history is often overlooked in the shadow of his son's many accomplishments as a warlord. Despite his leadership shortcomings, without Nobutora's work laying both military and economic foundation for Shingen's massive military campaigns, his son's successes might not have been as extensive as they were.

*Saga of the Samurai: Book 3*

## TAKEDA SHINGEN: THE STRUGGLE BEGINS
### THE KAI TAKEDA 3 (1521-1548)

Book 3 in this series tells the story of Shingen's early years, including his military and diplomatic relations with the Suwa, Murakami, Ogasawara, and Imagawa families. Sixteen pages of color plates, maps, and illustrations paint a vivid image of Shingen's life during these years.

# UPCOMING TITLES IN THE SAGA OF THE SAMURAI SERIES

*Saga of the Samurai: Book 5*

## SHINGEN - THE CONQUEROR
### THE KAI TAKEDA 5 (1559-1568)

Book 5 in the series will continue to follow the life of Shingen and his campaigns in Shinano and Kôzuke.

For more information and comments on
The Saga of the Samurai series, be sure to visit

## WWW.SAGAOFTHESAMURAI.COM